SOCIAL PSYCHOLOGY

DIFFERENT ASPECTS

(A COMPENDIUM OF SELECTED RESEARCH PAPER AND ARTICLES)

SOCIAL PSYCHOLOGY

DIFFERENT ASPECTS

(A COMPENDIUM OF SELECTED RESEARCH PAPER AND ARTICLES)

Edited by:

Dr. Gurvir Singh

M.Phil., NET & Ph. D. Physical Education

Assistant Professor, Department of Physical Education,

A.S. College, Khanna. Ludhiana.

red'shine
Publication
INDIA

SOCIAL PSYCHOLOGY: DIFFERENT ASPECTS

Edited by: Dr. Gurvir Singh

■

RED'SHINE PUBLICATION PVT. LTD.

Headquarters (India): 88-90 REDMAC, Navamuvada,

Lunawada, India-389 230

Contact: +91 76988 26988

Registration no. GJ31D0000034

In Association with,

RED'MAC INTERNATIONAL PRESS & MEDIA. INC

India | Sweden | UK

■

Text © *Dr. Gurvir Singh*, 2022

Cover page ©RED'SHINE Studios, Inc, 2022

■

■

ISBN: 978-93-93239-80-8

ISBN-10: 93-93239-80-0

DIP: 18.10.9393239800

DOI: 10.25215/9393239800

Price: ₹ 400

May, 2022 (First Edition)

■

■

www.redshine.co.in | info@redshine.in

Printed in India | Title ID: 9393239800

PREFACE

The field of social psychology has traditionally been described as a bridge between psychology and sociology. Social psychology focuses on the importance of individual or social influences on a person's perception of the world around them. There are some important differences in the way that *psychological* social psychologists and *sociological* social psychologists approach the field of study. Most notably, *psychological* social psychologists focus on individuals' mental processes, while *sociological* social psychologists focus on societal factors. Social psychology is the scientific study of how we think about, feels about and behave toward the people in our lives and how our thoughts, feelings, and behaviours are influenced by those people. The science of social psychology began when scientists first started to systematically and formally measure the thoughts, feelings, and behaviours of human beings. Social psychology concerns the interplay between the individual person and the social situation. The social situation refers to the other people we interact with every day. The key aspect of the social situation is that the people around us produce social influence, or the processes through which other people change our thoughts, feelings, and behaviours, and through which we change theirs. Social influence operates largely through social norms. People also desire to affiliate with others, a motive known as other-concern, and doing so is an important part of human behaviour. An important source of our common human experiences is our culture- a group of people, normally living within a given geographical region, who share a common set of social norms. Norms in Western cultures are primarily oriented toward individualism and self-concern, whereas norms in East Asian cultures are more focused on collectivism and other-concern. The overarching goal of psychology is to understand the behaviour, mental functions, and emotional processes of human beings. This field ultimately aims to benefit society, partly through its focus on better understanding of mental health and mental illness. Psychologists study many different areas, including biological foundations, mental well-being, change and development over time, the self and others, and potential dysfunctions. They explore how psychological factors interact with biological and socio-cultural factors to influence individual development. Psychologists attempt to understand not only the role of mental functions in individual and social behaviour, but also the physiological and biological processes that underlie cognitive functions and behaviours.

Social perception allows individuals to make judgments and form impressions about other people. These judgments are primarily based on observation, although pre-existing knowledge influences how observed information is interpreted. "Social perception" refers to the first stages in which people process information in order to determine another individual's or group's mind-set and intentions. These early stages help us interpret each other's actions so that additional information can be quickly inferred in order to predict behaviour. Social perceptions can influence an individual's behaviours and attitudes. Professional sportsmen are recognised for the stress and strain that they put their bodies through and it is widely accepted that they will encounter physical injury at some point. There is a societal view that sport is about winning and competing, and the focus is predominantly about individual or team performance. The fields of sports psychology and sports psychiatry are rapidly developing areas aimed at understanding, diagnosing, treating and rehabilitating athletes. Social and psychological problems are not new phenomena to India. There were problems in India before independence and after independence these problems were also continue to grow. Sport Psychology provides a fundamental understanding of how the various aspects of psychology can be applied to sport participation.

Dr. Gurvir Singh

CONTENTS

1

SOCIAL PSYCHOLOGICAL AND PERSONAL CAUSES OF LACK OF PARTICIPATION OF FEMALE STUDENTS IN SPORTS

Dr. Gurvir Singh [1]

Abstract

The present study was to find out the social, psychological and personal causes of lack of participation of female students in sports. The sample size of 100 individuals was collected from the colleges of Ludhiana. The respondents were randomly selected from colleges affiliated to Panjab University Chandigarh. Self made questionnaire wes used. The results have revealed that female students face more psychological problems comparison to social and personal problems.

Since ages, female students continue to feel to be a weaker section of society. Biologically it can be said that this may be true that, female students is not as strong as man, but being physically weak does not mean that she should be sealed within the four walls of her home, limited herself to her biological role resulting in life long dependence on men. Games and sports are old as human society and have achieved an universal following in the modern times. These have become integral part of education process. Millions of people take part in sports of educational process. Recreational purpose or for health, strength and fitness and for displaying superiority over other in

---

[1] Assistant Professor, Department of Physical Education, A.S. College Khanna.

competition sports. Some competitive games and sports are taking shape of a profession with high skills, and with ample benefits linked with high degree of popularity.

Championship performances no longer occur at random or as a result of chance alone. International sports and games are influenced by many factors such as level of physical, physiological, physiological abilities; nutrition, technique, tactics physique, body size and body composition.

Historically speaking women and female students have enjoyed a low status of female students was relative high, such as Egyptian, Minoan and sports the women or upper class participated extensively in variety of physical activities. However in classical Athens their status was low and their participatory role was similarly low while in roman world women was status vacillated and their activities reflected the social norms. Thaw a few women and their activities reflected the social norms, though few women participated in sports in ancient Greece yet they were not permitted to participate in the Olympics and even to witness the Olympic games. It was prohibited for women to enter the stadium.

Those who broke the rules, the law and yet escaped the punishment was kallipateria who happened to be daughter, sister and mother of Olympics heroes. She brought her son Olympia to complete her self disguised, in recognition of the meritorious performance of her father, brother and lastly her son let her free unpunished. The orthodox view about female students in sports is that when compared with males, females have always held and continue to hold, an inferior position in sporting achievement.

Myths and attitude that female students are physically, physiologically, socially and physiologically weaker are fading way slowly. Now women are even president and prime minister of status and hold very high posts in recent. Olympics the mass media discovered female students sports and there has been even growing phenomenon featuring such great athletes as Olga korbut, Nadia Comaneci, Nancy and many other girls and female students are entering more and more sports.

Most people in industrialized would rephrase the positive aspects of sports dramatized and reinforce the value defined as important in their own cultures. However, if ask these questions to people in society in sports, the answer would very widely. Some would emphasize the negative and agent in change of society. This can confusing for someone locking for a single correct answer.

An understanding of sociological theories is especially import for anyone interested in bringing about socially change. With the help of theories it is possible to develop idea about how the socially world operates and how certain change might affect the operation. Throughout the world the functionalist approach has been used to make numerous decisions about sports program at both the national and local level. It has encouraged the development and growth organized youth; sports program in high school and collages the growth of sports opportunities for girl and female students the use of sports in military training and promotion of the Olympic games as Since ages, female students continue to feel to be a weaker section of society. Biologically it can be said that this may be true that, female students is not as strong as man, but being physically weak does not mean that she should be sealed within the four walls of her home, limited herself to her biological role resulting in life long dependence on men. The very thought of all (his creates psychological problems in female students) Inspire of control over birth and with opportunities thrown open to her in various fields along with some lab our savings gadgets in the house, she still seeks a place as an independent honorable human being contributing to the onward march of humanity. The concept of equality has exercised a powerful emotional appeal in the struggle of female students to free themselves from the age-old oppression. A women's working status is, no doubt, a key 10 social independence. But it is to be explored as yet that to what extent has the society accepted and approved the changed status of female students a men of trying to maintain international goodwill.

Sexual harassment of women in ground is an important instance of the oppression of women, Padavic and Reskin (1990) indicated that the women experienced sexual harassment, paternalism and functional differentiation at the hands of their male co-workers and supervisors. This experience did not stop the female students from doing their work, though it did affect their enjoyment of the jobs and had a minor influence on their interest in accepting permanent positions. It is a part and parcel of a systematic and consistent strategy of men to dominate.

They have to face a number of problems in every sphere of life which can be categorized under different heads like psychological problems, adjustment problems, social problems, economic problems, marital problems and biological problems. Woman has been a victim of problems like wife-beating, dowry-death, sati etc. it is also found that men do not adopt ambivalence object to their social and economic freedom. Marriage and family is still considered as for female students. The notion or belief of Indian people that a female students has to play the role of a housewife or a mother and nothing beyond that is very hard to change. They fear that education of girls and then their going out on jobs might alienate them from their traditional roles and lead to conflicts and maladjustment. Thus they have to face many adjustment problems.

Poverty of Indian people also creates many more problems of female students. Many people can not afford to provide education and games yet prefer to educate their male offspring but think it a wastage to invest on girls. In modern society women need to educate both to earn and live richer and fuller life. This is only possible if the women gets higher education or higher achievements in sports. To enable a women to make her unique contribution to the society, all her physical, metal and spiritual potentialities must be fully developed. Women education or games holds a key to the development of families and of the, society at large.

It is always the woman in our society who comes to a new environment after getting married and faces adjustment problems it can not be said that adjustment problems arise only from outside the home i.e. in ground, but the problem is very much (here inside the four walls of home itself. It is always the female students who has to adjust herself to the new style of life. She has to deal with new family, as well as with society and tries o win at all fronts. If she gets help from them, then she adjusts well and easily otherwise she becomes psychologically disturbed. Women health complications also and are likely to get more diseases than men. Right from the age of puberty, she faces lots of health problems. D'Arcy and Siddique (1985) reported that women showed to mental illness, including lack of social integration, overload of household chores, economic dependency on their husbands, not working in paid jobs, and poor quality of family life.

Objectives

1. Study the social causes of lack of participation in sports by female at college level.
2. To reveal the personal causes related to lack of participation of female at college level.
3. To examine Psychological causes related to lack of participation of female at college level.

Hypothesis

1. There is no significant difference between social and personal problems of female students in sports.
2. There is significant difference between social and psychological problems of female students in sports.
3. There is no significant difference between social and personal problems of female students in sports.

Delimitations

1. The study was delimited to Ludhiana district only.
2. The study was delimited to co-education and women degree colleges only.
3. The study was delimited to active female players of under college level, national level and international level.

Methodology

The sample size from the 100 from Ludhiana district. The respondents were randomly selected from four colleges affiliated to Panjab university Chandigarh. Self made questionnaire was used.

Tools

An information sheet pertaining to age, game, level of game and residential was prepared by the investigator.

A questionnaire consisting of social, personal and psychological problems was prepared. There were five options i.e Strongly Agree, Agree, Undecided, Disagree and Strongly Disagree respectively for each statement.

Statistical techniques

Mean, SD, t-test were applied to know the differences among the various groups under study.

Results and Discussion
Social, Psychological and Personal causes of lack of participation of female students in sports

Table 4.1: Comparison of Social, Psychological and Personal Problems of Female Students

Problems	N	Mean	SD	SEM
Social	100	102.61	50.60	5.06
Personal	100	31.90	9.32	0.93
Psychological	100	107.55	25.71	2.57

The result shows that mean score of social problem has been found to be 102.61, SD 50.60, SEM 5.06. Where as the mean score of the personal problem of sports women has been found to be 31.90, SD 9.32 and SEM 0.93 where as the mean score of the psychological problem of sports women have been found to be 107.55 SD 25.71 and SEM 2.57. This indicates that the intensity of psychological problems of sports women is higher than social and personal problems.

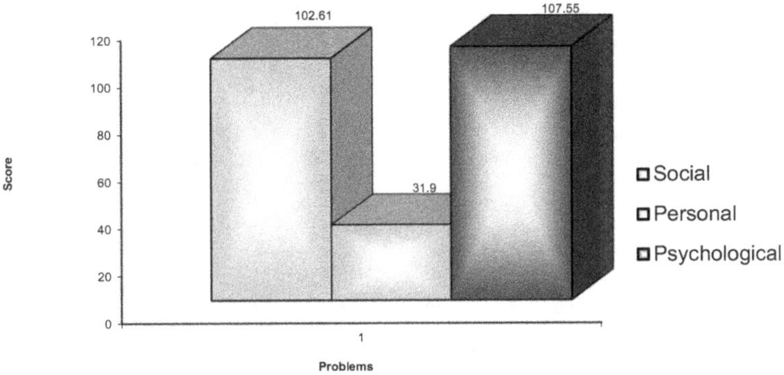

Graph 4.1: Comparison of Social, Psychological and Personal Problems of Female Students

Table 4.2: Comparison of Social and Personal Problems of Female Students

Problems	N	Mean	SD	SEM	df	t
Social	100	102.61	50.60	5.06	198	**
Personal	100	31.90	9.32	0.93		13.74

*   Significant at 0.05

**   Significant at 0.01

The 't' value at 198 df for 0.05 and 0.01 level of confidence are 1.96 and 2.60 from the above table, it is clear that 't' value is found to be significant at 0.01 level of significant. Thus, the hypotheses, namely "There is no significant difference between social and personal problems of female students in sports" is rejected. It is clear from the mean scores that female students have scored more on social problems than personal problems.

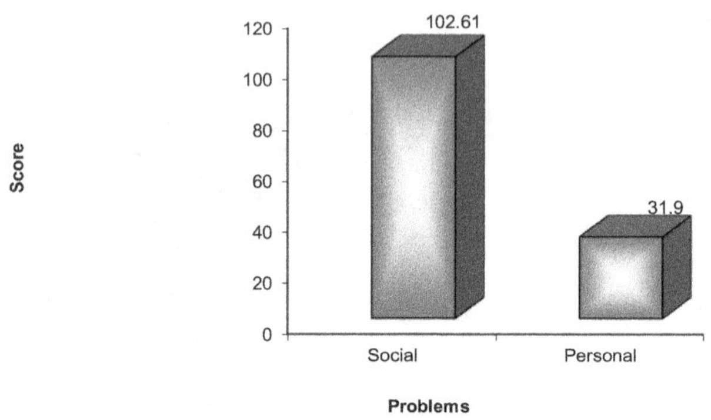

Graph 4. 2: Comparison of Social and Personal Problems of Female Students

SOCIAL AND PSYCHOLOGICAL CAUSES OF LACK OF PARTICIPATION OF FEMALE STUDENTS IN SPORTS

Table 4.3: Comparison of Social and Psychological Problems of Female Students

Problems	N	Mean	SD	SEM	df	t
Social	100	102.61	50.60	5.06	198	*
Psychological	100	107.55	25.71	2.57		0.870

*   Significant at   0.05

**   Significant at   0.01

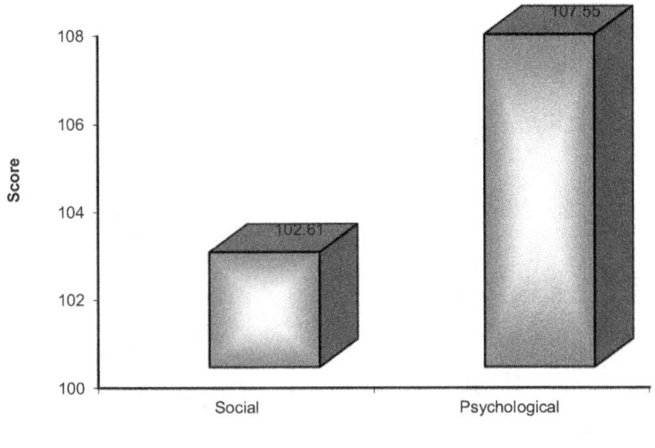

Graph 4.3: Comparison of Social and Psychological Problems of Female Students

PERSONAL AND PSYCHOLOGICAL CAUSES OF LACK OF PARTICIPATION OF FEMALE STUDENTS IN SPORTS

Table 4.3: Comparison of Social and Psychological Problems of Female Students

Problems	N	Mean	SD	SEM	df	t
Social	100	102.61	50.60	5.06	198	*
Psychological	100	107.55	25.71	2.57		0.870

*   Significant at 0.05

**   Significant at 0.01

The 't' value at 198 df for 0.05 and 0.01 level of confidence are 1.96 and 2.60 from the above table , it is clear that 't' value is found to be significant at 0.01 level of significant. Thus , the hypotheses, namely " There is significant difference between social and psychological   problems of female students in sports" is accepted.

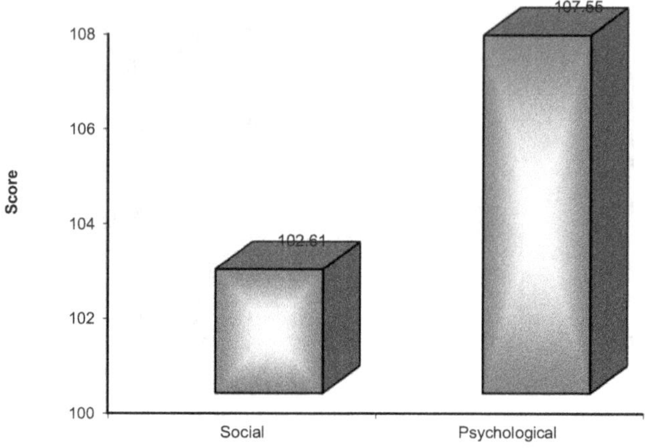

Graph 4.3: Comparison of Social and Psychological Problems of Female Students

PERSONAL AND PSYCHOLOGICAL CAUSES OF LACK OF PARTICIPATION OF FEMALE STUDENTS IN SPORTS

Table 4.4: Comparison of Personal and Psychological Problems of Female Students

Problems	N	Mean	SD	SEM	Df	t
Personal	100	31.90	9.32	0.93	198	**
Psychological	100	107.55	25.71	2.57		27.66

*   Significant at   0.05

**   Significant at   0.01

The 't' value at 198 df for 0.05 and 0.01 level of confidence are 1.96 and 2.60 from the above table, it is clear that 't' value is found to be significant at 0.01 level of significant. Thus, the hypotheses, namely "There is no significant difference between social and personal problems of female students in sports" is rejected. It is clear from the mean scores that female students have scored more on social problems than personal problems.

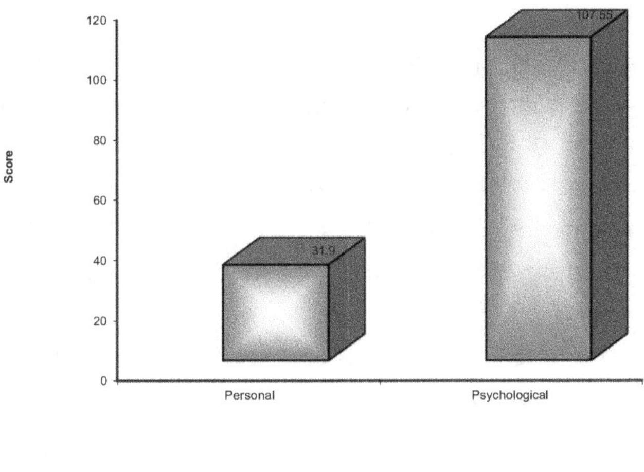

Graph 4.4: Comparison of Personal and Psychological Problems of Female Students

Conclusion

Social, Psychological and Personal problems

1. The research shows that mean score of social problems of female students is higher then the mean sore of personal problem of female students. This indicated that the intensity of social problems of female students is higher than personal problems.

2. Result shows that the intensity of psychological of female students is higher than the social problems.

3. Result shows that the intensity of the psychological of female students is higher than the personal problems.

4. After comparing the score of social problems, personal problems and psychological problems is more as compared to their variables.

Bibliography

1. Akabas, S.H. (1988) Women, Work and Mental Health: Room for improvement, *Journal of Primary Prevention.* Fal Win; Vol. 9(1-2) 130-140.
2. Cantelon et al, (1982) Sport, culture and modern state, University of Toronto Press, Toronto (collection of articles representing critical analysis of the relationship between sport and society.
3. Chandra SS (2004) Sociology of education. *Atlantic publishers and distribution.*
4. Chikodikar, S.S. (1992) Women in white collar jobs. *A study in Social Change with Special Reference to Kolhapur city.* Unpublished report, Kolhapur, Shivaji University.
5. Coakey, 1986 Sports in Society, Printed in the United States of America .
6. Dail, P.W. (1986) Problems of Socialization: Women and Men working Together International Sociological Association (ISA).
7. Dass, S.P. (1982) The Status of Indian Women New Delhi: E.S.S. Publications 92 pp.
8. Ghadially, R, Kumar, P. (1989) Stress, strain and copying styles of female professionals, *Indian Journal of Applied Psychology.* Jan; Vol 26 (1) 1-8.
9. Gray, J.D. (1980) Counseling women who want both a profession and a family. *Personnel and Guidance Journal.* Sep. Vol 59(1) 43-6.
10. Kalpana Debnath, (1994) Women's performance and sports. *Friends publications.*
11. Miller, H.A. (1990) Earning bread and baking bread: Reconciling worklife and familylife. Employee Assistance Quarterly. Vol 5(4) 83-88.

12. Morgan, W. (1985) Radical social theory of sport: A critique and a conceptual emendation.

13. Navare, S. (1990) *The role of Education in Socialization of Schedule Caste Women- A case study of Primary School teachers in Pune.* A dissertation submitted to the University Poona for the degree of Ph.D. in Education.

14. Renick, J.C. (1980) Sexual harassment at work: Why it happens, what to do about it. *Personnel Journal.* Aug; Vol 59(8) 658-662.

15. Roy, L. Suresh et al, (2006) Psychological profile of National level fencers of India. *Journal of sports and sports science.* Oct. 2006, Vol 29(4) p-17.

16. Singh Adaraspal, (2007) Exploration of anxiety among school children. *Journal of sports and sports science.* Oct. 2007, Vol 30(4) p-17.

2

SPORTS PSYCHOLOGY- IS A HEALTHY WAY OF LIVING LIFE FOR STRESS MANAGEMENT

Kayjeet Singh [1]

ABSTRACT

Stress is a common problem that affects almost all of us at some point in our lives. Learning to identify when you are under stress, what is stressing you, and different ways of coping with stress can greatly improve both your mental and physical well being. This course provides you with some basic information on stress and some simple recommendations for dealing with stress. It is not intended to take the place of advice from a physician or counselor, but it can be the first step in deciding how to manage your stress and increase your well being. The index below lists the different sections of this course. To take the course and learn more about stress management, click on the link at the bottom of this page titled "Begin: Class I: What is Stress?" As you continue, each section of the course will link to the next section at the bottom of the page. If you have any questions about this course, about stress management in general, or about other services offered by the Mountain State Centers for Independent Living, contact the center nearest you. The information and advice in these courses are never intended to take the place of advice from a trained physician, medical worker, or counselor. Before beginning any new exercise, diet, or lifestyle changes it is always best to consult your primary care provider.

[1] Ph.D., Research Scholar, Department of Physical Education, Punjabi University, Patiala, Punjab, India

Keywords: *Yoga, Healthy, Living Life, Stress Management, Asanas, Symptoms.*

INTRODUCTION
Stages of stress

Stress is a Sudden Biological Change. It has become the curse of 21st century and is silent killer in the modern world. Stress is the greatest danger to the information era. Stress is the priceless poison for human life in the universe. It can disturb any one's physical, mental, emotional and behavioral balance. Stress can damage different parts of human body from muscles from tissues to organs and blood vessels. It can speed up pulse rate and respiration. It can raise blood pressure and body temperature. It can also interfere with the body metabolism, digestion, appetite, sleep, sexuality and even fertility. Occupational stress includes the environmental factors or stressors such as work overload, role ambiguity, role conflict and poor working conditions associated with a particular job. There are three stages a person goes through while suffering from stress. Know more about them.

Alarm stage

This stage experiences an over acting of the sympathetic nervous system wherein adrenaline and cortisol increase and blood flows away from the brain to the muscles. As a result, dendrites shrink back in the brain to moderate the flow of information, slowing or closing down the nonessential body functions. The whole body starts preparing itself to fight against the reason of stress. The fear, excitement or pressure is evident on the sufferer's face.

Resistance stage

In this stage, the body keeps making continuous efforts to cope with stress and therefore feels run down and the person starts feeling irritated, over reacts to minor situations and gets mentally and physically weak. Psychological, physical and behavioral changes are also clearly visible.

Exhaustion stage

If a student is preparing for his exam and despite of every possible effort, he is not able to relate to his studies, he is bound to get stressed. The stress could reach a height where he/she may feel completely exhausted and helpless to the extent of committing suicide. This is the exhaustion stage. This stage is further divided into two phases: The nature of stress is broadly of two types- Eustress (Positive stress, Distress (Negative stress).

The positive effects of pressure: Sometimes, however, the pressures and demands that may cause stress can be positive in their effect. One example of this is where sportsmen and women flood their bodies with fight-or-flight adrenaline to power an explosive performance. Another example is where deadlines are used to motivate people who seem bored or unmotivated. We will discuss this briefly here, but throughout the rest of this site we see stress as a problem that needs to be solved.

The negative effects of pressure: In most work situations jobs, our stress responses cause our performance to suffer. A calm, rational, controlled and sensitive approach is usually called for in dealing with most difficult problems at work: Our social inter-relationships are just too complex not to be damaged by an aggressive approach, while a passive and withdrawn response to stress means that we can fail to assert our rights when we should.

Signs and Symptoms of Stress

If exposure to stressors continues for a longer period of time, chronic health problems can develop, such as:

Psychological and emotional	Cognitive
• Feeling heroic, invulnerable, euphoric	• Memory problems
• Denial	• Disorientation
• Anxiety and fear	• Confusion
• Worry about safety of self and others	• Slowness of thinking and comprehension
• Anger	• Difficulty calculating, making

Psychological and emotional	Cognitive
	decisions
• Irritability	• Poor concentration
• Restlessness	• Limited attention span
• Sadness, grief, depression, moodiness	• Loss of objectivity
• Distressing dreams	• Unable to stop thinking about the disaster
• Guilt or "survivor guilt"	• Blaming
• Apathy	
• Identification with survivors	

Behavioral	Physical
• Change in activity	• Increased heartbeat, respiration
• Decreased efficiency and effectiveness	• Increased blood pressure
• Difficulty communicating	• Upset stomach, nausea, diarrhea
• Increased sense of humor	• Change in appetite, weight loss or gain
• Outbursts of anger, frequent arguments	• Sweating or chills
• Inability to rest or "letdown"	• Tremors (hands, lips)
• Change in eating habits	• Muscle twitching
• Change in sleeping patterns	• "Muffled" hearing
• Change in patterns of intimacy, sexuality	• Tunnel vision
• Change in job performance • Periods of crying	• Feeling uncoordinated • Headaches
• Increased use of alcohol, tobacco, or drugs	• Soreness in muscles
• Social withdrawal, silence	• Lower back pain
• Vigilance about safety or environment	• Feeling a "lump in the throat"
• Avoidance of activities or trigger memories	• Exaggerated startle reaction
• Proneness to accidents	• Fatigue • Menstrual cycle changes
	• Change in sexual desire
	• Decreased resistance to infection
	• Flare-up of allergies and arthritis
	• Hair loss

Yoga & Meditation for Stress Relief

Yoga is most Recognized form of Exercise, Stretching, Aerobic exercise and Meditation. The definition of yoga is "to yoke or joint together" it integrates the mind and body focusing on balance posture, deep breathing, stretching and relaxation. Yoga evolved from of the Hindu, Jaina, and Buddhist religious traditions in India. Yoga alters stress response and person's attitude, towards stress along with improving self confidence, increasing one's sense of well being, and creating a feeling of relaxation and calmness

Yoga is an ancient art that is defined as the union of the soul with God. It is "a path of personal spiritual development that utilizes meditation to bring enlightenment, self-realization, and, ultimately, the attainment of God and bliss". Originally, the ultimate goal of yoga was called Samadhi, or self-realization.

Patanjali is father of yoga around the sixth century B.C. appeared in the massive epic The Mahabharata written by sage Vyasa and containing The Bhagavad Gita. Krishna explains to Arjuna about the essence of Yoga as practiced in daily lives ('Song of the Lord'), uses the term "yoga" extensively in a variety of ways. In addition to an entire chapter dedicated to traditional yoga practice, including meditation, it introduces three prominent types of yoga:

Karma yoga: The yoga of action

Bhakti yoga: The yoga of devotion, note Krishna had also specified devotion itself was action similar to above.

Jnana yoga: The yoga of knowledge. Patanjali introduced - Ashtanga or Power yoga - a more demanding workout where you constantly move from one posture to another ("flow").The dimensions of yoga are:-

• Yama (restraint)	• Dhyana (meditation)
•Niyama (healthy observances)	• Samadhi (higher consciousness)
• Asana (postures)	
• Pranayama (breathing)	
• Pratyahara (sensory withdrawal)	
• Dharana (concentration)	

Types of Asanas (postures)

They work at the chitta (subtle aspect of consciousness) level that eliminates the physical and mental tensions. They are trained in supine and prone position of the body respectively. Shavasana and Makarasana, Vijrasana, Bhujangasana, Trikonasana, Virabdrasana, Pranayama, Siddhasana with Kumbhaka, Padmasana, Yogamudras are important relaxative asanas

Benefits of Yoga
Mental calmness

Yoga asana practice is intensely physical. Concentrating so intently on what your body is doing has the effect of bringing calmness to the mind. Yoga also introduces you to meditation techniques, such as watching how you breathe and disengagement from your thoughts, which help calm the mind.

Stress reduction

Physical activity is good for relieving stress, and this is particularly true of yoga. Because of the concentration required, your daily troubles, both large and small, seem to melt away during the time you are doing yoga. This provides a much-needed break from your stressors, as well as helping put things into perspective. The emphasis yoga places on being in the moment can also help relieve stress, as you learn not to dwell on past events or anticipate the future. You will leave a yoga class feeling less stressed than when you started. Read more about yoga for stress management here.

Body awareness

Doing yoga will give you an increased awareness of your own body. You are often called upon to make small, subtle movements to improve your alignment. Over time, this will increase your level of comfort in your own body. This can lead to improved posture and greater selfconfidence.

CONCLUSION

Actually yoga combines several techniques to combat stress. Yoga provides a combination of benefits such as breathing exercises, stretching exercises, fitness program, and meditation practice and guided meditations all in one technique. That is powerful, that is very powerful! Even for people who have physical limitations yoga can be very beneficial just by practicing the breathing techniques, the meditation and the guided meditation. Just by doing this you can have great benefits with the practice of yoga. So in conclusion yes yoga can be a great remedy for stress and can offer some stress relief. Yoga has combined set of principles and exercises that can greatly benefit you and help you to deal with stress.

References

1. Cooper CL, Marshall J (1976) Occupational sources of stress: a review of the literature relating to coronary heart disease and mental ill-health, Journal of Occupational and Organizational physiology 49: 11-28.
2. Taylor, Matthew J, M.P.T, R.Y.T (2003) "Yoga Therapeutics: An Ancient Dynamic Systems Theory" Techniques is orthopedics 18: 115-125.
3. Malathi A, Damodaran A (1999) Stress due to exams in medical students–role of yoga. Indian J Physiol Pharmacol 43: 218-224.
4. Anand S (2000) The Essence of the Hindu Religion. Los Angeles, CA: ASK Publications.

3

MUSIC AND SPORTS PERFORMANCE

Neha Kashyap[1], Ravi Kumar[2], Ruhi[3]

ABSTRACT:

Research shows that music can effect arousal regulation (Lukas, n.d.; Nilsson, Unosson, & Rawal, 2005), motivation (Karageorghis & Terry, 1997), and mood levels (Gfeller, 1988). Research has also shown that music can help enhance athletic performance (Dorney & Goh, 1992; Karageorghis & Terry, 1997; Krumhansl, 2002). Although a great amount of research exists that examines music in sport, little research has been found that examines this phenomenon from an existential phenomenological perspective. The current research examined the experience of music in sport. The results suggest athletes utilize music for arousal regulation, concentration, mood enhancement, and team cohesion.

INTRODUCTION:

Music plays a central role in people's everyday lives (Rentfrow & Gosling, 2003). Research shows that music can affect arousal regulation (Lukas, n.d.; Nilsson, Unosson, & Rawal, 2005), motivation (Karageorghis & Terry, 1997), and mood levels (Gfeller, 1988). Research has also shown that music can be a facilitator to athletic performance (Dorney & Goh, 1992; Karageorghis & Terry, 1997; Krumhansl, 2002). For instance, music affects mood states by eliciting a certain emotional response while listening to a song (Dorney & Goh, 1992).

---

[1] (PET) JNV School, Kargil (J&K)
[2] Research scholar, Punjabi University, Patiala
[3] Student, Guru Nanak Dev University, Amritsar

Moreover, research has shown that music allows athletes to disassociate from feelings of fatigue and perceived exertion rates (Karageorghis & Terry, 1997).The use of music to enhance sports performance has been of deep interest for two decades. Music is essentially the organization of five primary elements: melody, harmony, tempo, rhythm, and dynamics. *Melody* is the tune of a piece of music, the part to which you might hum or whistle along. *Harmony* acts to shape the mood of the music to make you feel happy, sad, soulful or romantic through the meshing of sounds. *Tempo* is the speed at which music is played and is measured in beats per minute (bpm). *Rhythm* refers to the way music is accented and combines with tempo to make people instinctively move in time with it. *Dynamics* have to do with the energy transmitted by musicians through touch or breathe to influence the volume of their instruments. History reveals that from the dawn of civilization, ancient cultures combined sounds in ways that affected the human psyche. As time progressed, primitive forms of music evolved into ever more structured and artistically pleasing arrangements. Music became common in many types of activity: worship, education, entertainment, healing, and not least, athletic performance. It seems unlikely that music will ever be on the list banned substances published by the International Olympics Committee, and of course, music does not carry the same risks as other ergogenic aids.

MUSIC IN OLYMPIC GAMES:

Music was incorporated into the ancient Olympics games where rhythmic clapping and drumming accompanied some of the events. The modern Olympics games have continued to formalize the association between music and athletic endeavour. Music is an integral part of some of the Olympics events such as rhythmic gymnastics and synchronized swimming. Live music also features prominently at the opening and closing ceremonies of the games.

DISSOCIATION AND MOOD EFFECTS:

Music may influence physical performance by narrowing the attention, which may divert it from feelings of fatigue during training or competition. Music can make training and endurance activities seem less hard. Music can increase work output and enhance the emotional experience of physical activity by blocking out the negative sensations associated with physical exertion and fatigue. Scientists commonly refer to focus on music for its reputed distraction effect as a dissociation technique. Some athletes hum, whistles or sing their preferred music to dissociate from a tough workout.

AROUSAL CONTROL:

Music can influence performance by altering arousal levels; it can be used as a legal stimulant or sedative prior to and during competition. Music affects arousal levels for at least two reasons. First, physiological processes tend to react to the rhythmic components of music; fast upbeat music increase respiration rate, heart rate, sweat secretion, and other indicators of physical activation. Second; arousal is increased through extra musical associations; in other words, the music promotes thoughts that inspire either physical activity or heroic deeds. Just as the association between your first love and "your song" can be very strong, so is the relationship between music and sporting endeavour.

SKILL LEARNING:

Think back to your days in elementary school when your first physical education classes were probably set to music. Music gave you opportunity to explore various planes of motion and to improve coordination skills through dance and play. Studies have consistently shown that application of purposefully selected music can have a positive effect on the style characteristics of movement in sports. A New Zealand-based study also looking at gymnastics found that music made learning skills more enjoyable while also promoting "greater freedom to bodily expression" and a "superior quality of movement presentation."

MUSIC FOR WORKOUT:

Most athletes use music for at least one of their weekly workout-usually gym based workout. Some gyms hold a licence to play music from a certain music supplier or a contracted to use a particular radio station. In present time most of the sports persons use to listen to the music during jogging and other warming up exercises. It makes the workout more enjoyable and easy.

MUSIC IN COMPETITION:

To use music effectively on the day of competition one should be very careful and should be aware of optimal level of arousal. Gentle music with powerful lyrics is ideal for keeping from bubbling over. In a team situation, a coach or team manager might create an entire music-related routine to prepare for the contest. Music program should be building up in such a way that as you switch off the last track you should be in an optimal psychological state to compete.

MUSIC FOR RELAXATION:

Music is also very helpful in revealing tension, psyching down, and aiding relaxation. Athletes are encouraged to use relaxing music on the eve of competition to relieve anxiety and aid's a restful night sleep. Listening to relaxing music between rounds of events or during the evenings at multiday championships is a great way to switch off and unwind. Selection of music tracks that would be suitable between rounds of an event might have a slow beat but inspirational lyrics to keep you in touch with the fact that more efforts will soon be required while keeping your body from expending energy unnecessarily. The music should be played on soothing, "warm" instruments such as strings, clarinet, or piano and its emotional qualities should be neutral or relaxing.

WHEN NOT TO USE MUSIC:

The human brain has limited capacity, and researchers have consistently shown that when music is combined with learning a difficult skill such as throwing events, it can slow down learning. Learning a new skill requires more concentration and more attention to the trainer or instructor, and listening to music can disturb the athlete's ability to concentrate on what they are learning. Similarly when a coach or teacher is giving instructions, music can be an unwanted distraction. If the movements are steady and rhythmic, the music should not have fluctuation in tempo.

CONCLUSION:

Music can be applied in many ways to training and competition, but until now, there have been no comprehensive guideline available to guide its effective use. It makes the difficult activity little easier and it is also helpful in learning the rhythmic activity easily. It also delays the onset of fatigue. In some situations use of music may be disadvantageous, such as in early stages of learning a complex skill. When you cycle on the road avoid music for the safety purpose.

REFERENCES:

1. Dosil, J. (Ed.). (2006). *The sport psychologist's handbook: A guide for sport-specific enhancement.* Chichester, UK: Wiley.

2. Gfeller, K. (1988). Musical components and styles preferred by young adults for aerobic fitness activities. *Journal of Music Therapy, 25* 28-43.

3. Honeybourne, J. (2006). *Acquiring skill in sport: An introduction.* New York: Routledge.

4. Lane, A.M. (Ed.) (2007). *Mood and human performance: Conceptual, measurement, and applied issues.* New York: Nova Science

5. Lukas, L. K. (n.d). Orthopedic outpatients' perception of perioperative music listening as therapy.*Journal of Theory Construction and Testing, 8(1), (7-12).*

6. Nilsson, U., Unosson, M., & Rawal, N. (2005). Stress reduction and analgesia in patients exposed to calming music postoperatively: A randomized controlled trial. *European Journal of Anesthesiology, 22* (96-102).

7. Smith, D., & Bar-Eli, M. (2007). *Essential readings in sports and exercise psychology.* Champaign, IL: Human Kinetics.

8. Wikipedia.org/wiki/Wikipedia

4

THE PSYCHOLOGY BEHIND MENTAL TOUGHNESS

Amanpreet Singh [1]

"Mental toughness is to see the long term gains rather than be put off by short term pains. Once you have this toughness, you have the winning edge" **Anonymous**

Introduction

Mental toughness is a collection of attributes that allow a person to persevere through difficult circumstances (such as difficult training or difficult competitive situations in games) and emerge without losing confidence. In recent decades, the term has been commonly used by

---

[1] Assistant Professor, Department of Education, D.A.V. College, Sec -10, Chandigarh

coaches, sport psychologists, sport commentators, and business leaders.

"Mental toughness" is keeping strong in the face of adversity. It's the ability to keep your focus and determination despite the difficulties you encounter. Events in our life rarely go the way we'd like them to, but that doesn't mean you have to let it throw you off your game. Mental toughness gives you the tenacity to learn from your mistakes without the devastating blow failure can sometimes deal. This resilience and fortitude also gives you the strength to keep emotions in check when something in your life seems overwhelming and you need to be strong. Essentially, mental toughness is the voice in the back of your head that tells you to keep going, keep pushing, and keep trying, even when the going gets tough. They say "life's tough, get a helmet." These tactics can help you create the helmet you need

What is Mental Toughness?

Mental Toughness describes the mind-set that every person adopts in everything they do. It is closely related to qualities such as character, resilience, grit, etc. It is defined as:

"Mental Toughness is a personality trait which determines in large part how people deal with challenge, stressors and pressure .... irrespective of prevailing circumstances"

Published research and case studies form around the world show that Mental Toughness is a major factor in:

Performance – explaining up to 25% of the variation in performance in individuals

Positive Behaviour – more engaged, more positive, more "can do"

Wellbeing – more contentment, better stress management , less prone to bullying

Aspirations - more ambitious, prepared to manage more risk

The '4Cs' model of mental toughness

Kobasa suggested that hardiness incorporates three key elements:

Control – the perceived ability of the individual to exert influence rather than experience helplessness;

Commitment – ie a refusal to give up easily;

Challenge – involving a person's ability to grow and develop rather than remain static, and to view change rather than stability as the norm.

Building on the work of Kobasa, the Hull team proposed that confidence (as well as control, commitment and challenge) was a key element of mental toughness. This has given rise to the '4Cs' model of mental toughness.

One researcher has proposed **four major influences** on toughening, as follows:

Early life experiences. Both human and animal studies have shown links between exposure to stressors in early life and reduced fear or emotionality when exposed to threats in adulthood;

Passive toughening. Intermittent exposure seems to protect against depletion of 'stress hormones' and is linked with their quicker returns to baseline levels. In other words, people become less sensitive and more tolerant of stress;

Active toughening. Physical fitness gained through aerobic conditioning is thought to be an important means of self-toughening. This could be related to the application of control;

Ageing. This has the opposite effects to the other three, tending to make people more sensitive to and less tolerant of stress.

Importance of mental toughness

An individual who is an average athlete and has mental toughness will be more successful than an individual who has natural talent but who is not mentally tough. This is because the mind is stronger than the body. Winners are not always determined by physical skill alone.

Becoming a mentally strong person takes practice and mindfulness. It requires tuning in to your bad habits and making a point of learning new habits to replace them. And sometimes it simply means learning to get out of your own way and let things happen.

The sports world provided one of the two main origins for the development of mental toughness and in many ways mental toughness and how it can impact is reasonably well understood by most coaches and trainers, the key areas are:

Performance – especially in competition and training work effectively and to a high standard

Positive Behaviour – developing a "can do" approach. If you think you can, you can. If you think you can't, you won't.

Wellbeing – feeling satisfied and motivated even when the going has been tough and there have been setbacks

Aspirations – being more ambitious.

Mentally tough athletes are more consistent than others. They don't miss workouts. They don't miss assignments. They always have their teammates back.

Methods to develop mental toughness

To develop and maintain the kind of mental toughness that success requires, it's crucial that you keep your thoughts and self-talk positive and avoid the habits that lead to negativity and unhealthy behaviours.

The strongest people are not those who show strength in front of us but those who win battles we never see them fight.

Help keep yourself prepared for whatever comes your way tomorrow by practicing good habits of mind and attitude:

1. ***Emotional stability***. Leadership often requires that you make good decisions under pressure. It's important that you maintain your capacity to stay objective and deliver the same level of performance regardless of what you're feeling.

2. ***Perspective***. Mental strength lets you carry on when the world seems to have turned against you. Learn to keep your troubles in proper perspective without losing sight of what you need to accomplish.

3. ***Readiness for change***. If change is truly the only constant, then flexibility and adaptability are among the most important traits you can develop.

4. ***Detachment***. You can get through setbacks and come out even stronger if you can remember that's it's not about you. Don't take things personally or waste time wondering Why me? Instead focus on what you can control.

5. ***Strength under stress***. Maintain resilience in the face of negative pressures by developing your capacity to deal with stressful situations.

6. ***Preparation for challenges.*** Life and business are filled with everyday demands, the occasional crisis, and unexpected twists. Make sure you have the resources to withstand the professional and personal crises that you'll sooner or later be facing.

7. ***Focus***. Keep your attention on the long-term outcomes to stay steady in the face of real or potential obstacles.

8. ***The right attitude toward setbacks***. Complications, unintended side effects, and complete failures are all part of landscape. Mitigate the damage, learn the lessons that will help you in the future, and move on.

9. ***Self-validation***. Don't worry about pleasing others: That's a hit-or-miss proposition for anyone but the worst sort of waffler. Instead, make a concentrated effort to do what is right and to know what you stand for.

10. ***Patience***. Don't expect results immediately or rush things to fruition before their time. Anything worthwhile takes hard work and endurance; view everything as a work in progress.

11. ***Control***. Avoid giving away your power to others. You are in control of your actions and emotions; your strength is in your ability to manage the way you respond to what is happening to them.

12. ***Acceptance***. Don't complain about the things you have no control over. Recognize that the one thing you can always

control is your own response and attitude, and use those attributes effectively.

13. ***Endurance in the face of failure***. View failure as an opportunity to grow and improve, not a reason to give up. Be willing to keep trying until you get it right.

14. ***Unwavering positivity***. Stay positive even -- especially -- when you encounter negative people. Elevate them; never bring yourself down. Don't allow naysayers to ruin the spirit of what you're accomplishing.

15. ***Contentment***. Don't waste time being envious of anyone else's car, house, spouse, job, or family. Instead be grateful for what you have. Focus on what you've achieved and what you're going to achieve instead of looking over your shoulder and being envious of what someone else has.

16. ***Tenacity***. It comes down to just three words: Never give up.

17. ***A strong inner compass***. When your sense of direction is deeply internalized, you never have to worry about becoming lost. Stay true to your course.

18. ***Uncompromising standards.*** Tough times or business difficulties aren't good reasons to lower the bar. Keep your standards high.

Developing your mental toughness can help you be more emotionally resilient, push you to go further and harder, and build armour to persevere against the bullets that life fires your way. It's not as easy to just "be tougher," though.

Maintaining Mental Toughness.

The maintenance of mental toughness occurred in the dimensional order of, attitude/mindset, training, competition, and post-competition. Coaches and sport psychologists stated that when strategies to maintain the subcomponents, 'belief' and 'focus' (attitude/mindset dimension) were perceived "to be in place", separate strategies could be introduced to maintain subcomponents in the training, competition, and post-competition dimensions. Mental skills that reenforced belief and focus, and encouraged the correct sport/life balance were highlighted as important in maintaining the attitude/mindset dimension. Other strategies involved extracting maximum value from successes, thereby enhancing greater awareness of the achievement of specific goals, "to increase focus and the durability of belief . . . to make it unshakable belief", and simulation training to increase the performer's belief that they could overcome any obstacle.

Effective communication and education regarding goals (e.g., retaining an Olympic title) and how they could be achieved, provided a justification for continuing in that sport, at that level. The development of process and performance goal 'maps' guided the performer through each step in achieving the long-term outcome goal and enhanced the performer's internal motivation to, "stick with the training and make achievement of his goal as the number one priority in his life". This increased focus and commitment, specifically in what they had to do day to day, encouraged competitiveness, and instilled pride in completing difficult sets. Other strategies included: developing competition routines; reactive practice; recognition of key moments in the game, and how to react to these; and simulation training, to incorporate all potential problems in games/races (e.g., mistakes, opponent's game plan)

Conclusion

Athletes are confronted with a variety of stressors, challenges, and adversities, external (e.g., hostile crowds, referee errors, challenged by an opponent, sport and life balance) and internal (e.g., fatigue, self-doubt, emotional instability), which are characteristic of the training and competition contexts of sport. Some athletes manage these demands or challenges positively, either having a smooth progression through the performance cycle or successfully negotiating these challenges in constructive ways. However, for other athletes, such demands or challenges can overwhelm their coping resources, creating major distress and negatively influencing their performance and goal attainment. What accounts for these individual differences in athletes' ability to manage both negatively (e.g., injury, deselection) and positively (e.g., winning streak, taking the lead in a match) construed challenges and demands? Most scholars, practitioners, and the general public suggest that the answer lies in an athlete's mental toughness.

Developing mental toughness is a process and it's not something you can conjure overnight. It takes a lot of patience and a conscious effort to become more resilient. Some things are bigger than all of us, but mental toughness can be your armour that glances the smaller blows away. If you have reasonable expectations, control over your emotions, strong motivation, and the patience to see things all the way through, you won't ever sweat the small stuff and you'll be better equipped to handle the big things in your life.

References:

1.   Bull, S. J., Shambrook, C. J., James, W., & Brooks, J. (2005). Towards an understanding of mental toughness in elite English cricketers. Journal of Applied Sport Psychology, 17(3), 209-227.
2.   Clough PJ, Earle K, Sewell D. (2002). Mental toughness: the concept and its measurement. In: Cockerill I., Solutions in sport psychology. London: Thomson; p. 32-43.
3.   Crust, L., and Azadi, K. (2010). Mental Toughness and Athletes' use of psychological strategies. European Journal of Sport Science, Volume 10, Issue 1, 43-51.

4. Drees, M. J., and Mack, M. G. (2012). An Examination of Mental Toughness over the Course of a Competitive Season. Journal of Sport Behavior, Vol. 35 (4), 377 – 386.

5. Golby, J., &Sheard, M. (2004). Mental toughness and hardiness at different levels of rugby league. Personality and Individual Differences, 37, 933-942. Goldberg, A. (2013). Concentration: the master skill of mental toughness. http://www.usaswimming.org/ViewNewsArticle.aspx?TabId= 1504&itemid= 5202&mid=9388

6. Gould, D., Dieffenbach, K., & Moffatt, A. (2002). Psychological characteristics and their development in Olympic champions. Journal of Applied Sport Psychology, 14, 172-204.

7. Gould, D., Hodge, K., Peterson, K., &Petlichkoff, L. (1987). Psychological foundations of coaching: Similarities and differences among intercollegiate wrestling coaches. The Sport Psychologist, 1, 293-308.

8. Gucciardi DF, Gordon S, Dimmock JA. (2008). Towards an understanding of mental toughness in Australian football. Journal of Applied Sport Psychology. 20:261-81.

9. Hanton, S., Evans, L., & Neil, R. (2003).Hardiness and the competitive trait anxiety response. Anxiety, Stress, and Coping, 16 (2), 167-184.

10. Harris, D.V and Harris, B.L. (1984).Concentration Grid Exercise. New York: Leisure Press.

11. Kuan G, Roy J. (2007). Goal profiles, mental toughness and its influence on performance outcomes among Wushu athletes. J Sports Sci Med.; 6:28-33. Mackenzie, B. (1997)Psychology[WWW] Available from: http://www.bria nmac.co.uk/psych.htm [Accessed 4/1/2014].

12. MadhuraIngalhalikar, Alex Smith, Drew Parker, Theodore D. Satterthwaite, Mark A. Elliott, KoshaRuparel, Hakon Hakonarson, Raquel E. Gur, Ruben C. Gur, and Ragini Verma. Sex differences in the structural connectome of the human brain. PNAS, December 2, 2013 DOI:

10.1073/pnas.1316909110 Mahoney MJ, Gabriel TJ, Perkins TS. (1987). Psychological skills and exceptional athletic performance. Sport Psychol.; 1:181-99.

13. Meyers MC, Bourgeois AE, LeUnes A, Murray NG. (1999). Mood and psychological skills of elite and sub-elite equestrian athletes. J Sport Behav.; 22:399-409.

14. Middleton, S.C., Marsh, H.M., Martin, A.J., Richards, G.E. and Perry, C. (2005) Discovering mental toughness: A qualitative study of mental toughness in elite athletes. Psychology Today, 22, 60-72

15. Middleton, S.C., Marsh, H.W., Martin, A.J., Richards, G.E., and Perry, C. (2005).Developing a Test for Mental Toughness: The Mental Toughness Inventory (MTI). Self-Research Centre. University of Western Sydney, Australia.

16. Newland, A., Newton, M., Finch, L., Harbke, C. R., and Podlog, L. (2013). Moderating variables in the relationship between mental toughness and performance in basketball. Journal of Sport and Health Science (2), 184-192. Nicholls, A. R., Polman, R. C., Levy, A. R., Backhouse, S. H. (2009). Mental toughness in sport: Achievement level, gender, age, experience, and sport type. Personality & Individual Differences, 47, 73-75.

17. Thelwell R, Weston N, Greenlees I. (2005). Defining and understanding mental toughness within soccer. Journal of Applied Sport Psychology, 17:326-32.

18. Thelwell, R. C., Such, B. A., Weston, N. J. V., Such, J. D., & Greenless, I. A. (2010). Developing mental toughness: Perceptions of elite female gymnasts. International Journal of Sport and Exercise Psychology, 8, 170- 189.

5

IMPORTANCE OF SPORTS FOR HEALTH, HEALTHY INDIVIDUAL AND HEALTHY SOCIETY

Kuljinder Singh [1]

Abstract:

Health and healthy human development is a necessary foundation for all development progress. Without healthy populations, the achievement of development objectives of healthy society will be out of reach. Physical exercise is increasingly being advocated as a means to maintain and enhance good physical, physiological and mental health.

Keywords: *Health, Development, Society, Sports.*

Introduction:

Health is the level of functional or metabolic efficiency of a living organism. In humans it is the ability of individuals or communities to adapt and self-manage when facing physical, mental or social challenges (Huber *et al.*, 2011). The current WHO definition of health, formulated in 1948, describes health as "a state of complete physical, mental and social well-being and not merely the absence of disease or infirmity" (WHO, 2006).

The health of individuals and populations is determined to a significant degree by social factors such as poverty, income inequality, education, employment, housing, gender and social connectedness. These social determinants of health produce

---

[1] Assistant Professor, Department of Sociology, A.S. College, Khanna.

widespread inequities in health within and between societies (Kelly, 2007).

Good health is fundamental to the ability of individuals to realize their full human potential. It is also a crucially important economic asset. Low levels of health impede people's ability to work and earn a living for themselves and their families. When someone becomes ill, an entire family can become trapped in a downward spiral of lost income and high health-care costs (Dodd and Cassels, 2006). On a national scale, poor population health diminishes productivity and impedes economic growth, while investment in better health outcomes is generally seen as an investment in economic growth.

The poor and disadvantaged experience worse health than the rich and powerful, have less access to services and die younger in all societies. Social factors have a direct impact on health status and must be addressed as part of any comprehensive health strategy. Sport's unique and universal power to attract, motivate and inspire makes it a highly effective tool for engaging and empowering individuals, communities and even countries to take action to improve their health. Physical activity is usually defined as "any bodily movement associated with muscular contraction that increases energy expenditure above resting levels". Physical activity, health and quality of life are closely interconnected. The human body was designed to move and therefore needs regular physical activity in order to function optimally and avoid illness.

At present there is sufficient evidence to show that those who live a physically active life can gain a number of health benefits, including the following: reduced risk of cardiovascular disease, prevention and/or delay of the development of arterial hypertension, and improved control of arterial blood pressure in individuals who suffer from high blood pressure, good cardio-pulmonary function, maintained metabolic functions and low incidence of type 2 diabetes, increased fat utilisation which can help to control weight, lowering the risk of obesity, a lowered risk of certain cancers, such as breast, prostate and colon cancer, improved mineralization of bones in young ages, contributing to the prevention of osteoporosis and fractures in older ages, improved digestion and regulation of the intestinal rhythm, maintenance and improvement in muscular strength and endurance, resulting in an increase in functional capacity to carry out activities of daily living, maintained motor functions including strength and balance, maintained cognitive functions and lowered risk of depression and dementia, lower stress levels and associated improved sleep quality, improved self-image and self-esteem and increased enthusiasm and optimism, decreased absenteeism (sick leave) from work, in very old adults, a lower risk of falling and prevention or delaying of chronic illnesses associated with ageing.

Children and young people take part in various kinds of physical activity, for example by playing games and participating in different sports. Sport and physical activity can make a substantial contribution to the well-being of people in developing countries. Exercise, physical activity and sport have long been used in the treatment and rehabilitation of communicable and non-communicable diseases. Physical activity for individuals is a strong means for the prevention of diseases and for nations is a cost-effective method to improve public health across populations.

Cardiovascular diseases

Cardiovascular diseases include coronary heart disease and stroke and are the leading causes of death globally. Causes of cardiovascular disease are unhealthy diets, physical inactivity and tobacco use. Physical activity reduces the risk of cardiovascular disease by improving glucose metabolism, reducing body fat and lowering blood pressure.

Physical exercise is a potent primary and secondary preventer of cardiovascular illness, particularly that due to ischemic heart disease. Evidence continues to accumulate that taking up exercise to prevent cardiovascular disease, or to reduce its risk of recurrence in those already affected by it, is efficacious and not associated with any appreciable harmful effects, if performed with appropriate safeguards (Adamu *et al.*, 2006).

Diabetes

Diabetes is a disease which occurs when body does not produce or properly use insulin and this may result in Type I or Type II diabetes. Diabetes may be prevented, or at least delayed, by weight loss, a healthy lifestyle, in particular, regular physical activity. Diet, drug therapy and physical activity are also major components of the treatment of diabetes, reducing the incidence and severity of obesity and the consequent risk of type 2 diabetes (obesity being more important than inactivity in the risk of developing type 2 diabetes) (Rana *et al.*, 2007).

Obesity

The lack of physical education in schools, limited access to safe play spaces and the growing use of electronic media are some contributors to this country-wide epidemic. Youth sports can get kids up and active, and help combat childhood obesity. Obesity is an abnormal accumulation of fat that may impair health and unlike other diseases, social and environmental factors play a significant role in defining obesity. The incidence of obesity is a growing concern internationally with an estimated more than 400 million obese people. The global rise in the incidence of obesity is related to a shift in diet and decreased physical activity levels.

Cancer

Cancer is not a single disease with a single type of treatment and in fact, there are over 200 types of cancer involving abnormal growth of cells in different parts of the body. It has been estimated that 40% of all cancers may be prevented by a healthy diet, physical activity and no tobacco use.

Mental health

One in four patients visiting a health service has at least one mental, neurological or behavioural disorder (such as depression, anxiety or mood disorders) that may not be diagnosed or treated. There is evidence to suggest that physical activity can reduce the symptoms of depression and can also be help to ameliorate mental well-being through improved mood and self-perception. When we are physically active, our mind is distracted from daily stressors, freeing us to think more creatively. Exercise reduces the levels of stress hormones in our body, such as adrenaline and cortisol. At the same time, it stimulates production of endorphins, which are natural mood lifters that can help lower our stress levels. Endorphins may even leave our feeling more relaxed and optimistic after a hard workout on the sports field.

Some unambiguous effects of sports activities in children

Physical activity is important to children's current and future health, and adherence to the physical activity guidelines produces a range of direct and indirect benefits. It assists in the control of body weight by increasing energy expenditure, this is important in teaching children and young people how to achieve a healthy 'energy balance', and avoid developing adult obesity. It reduces the risk of developing premature cardiovascular disease, type-2 diabetes, metabolic syndrome and some site specific cancers. Weight bearing physical activity is important in bone formation and remodelling. Beginning in the preschool years and continuing on to high school, children benefit immensely from playing sports. Not only sports as a source of fun and exercise for children, participating in sports can also lead to better cognitive and social skills. To encourage these benefits for all participants, competition must not be made the focus of children's sports.

Confidence

Children, who play sports gain confidence in their bodies and their ability to set goals, improve their skills and meet goals.

Children also become confident through having a reliable set of friends on their team and through working with an encouraging coach. The regular exercise that comes with playing sports can help boost confidence and improve self-esteem. As strength, skills, and stamina increase through playing sports, self-image will improve as well. Sports provide with a sense of mastery and control, which often leads to a feeling of pride and self-confidence. With the renewed vigor and energy that comes from physical activity, every child may be more likely to succeed in tasks off the playing field as well as on it.

Health

Children who play sports generally have stronger, healthier bodies than those who don't. They are more likely to be non-smokers and to maintain an appropriate body weight.

Academics

Exercise improves a child's memory and ability to focus, which tend to result in better learning skills and better performance in the classroom.

Kids and Sportsmanship

Kids are taught to be good sports. They must play fair, follow the rules, listen to officials and respect other players. After every baseball game, kids shake hands; tennis players approach the net also to shake hands and to maybe tell each other, "Good match." Kids witness boxers, who aim to knock each other out, touch gloves before each round. But for kids to develop a good attitude through playing sports, they need direction. Without it, kids could learn to cheat, taunt others and gloat.

Social Interaction

Playing team sports is a social activity, so by interacting with others you experience the benefits of social interaction. Not only can increased social interaction reduce stress and increase your mood, playing sports reduces social isolation and allows you an opportunity to make new friends and forget your worries while having fun with others.

Conclusion:

Above benefits of sports in reference to their effects on different physical, physiological and mental factors suggested that physical inactivity will become the norm, with significant threats to people's health as well as social and economic consequences. In present scenario, children today may die five years younger than their parents. "Designed to Move" is a worldwide campaign which, through collaborating with other organisations and existing programmes, is committed to integrating physical activity into everyday life and promoting the benefits of sport to ensure today's and tomorrow's generation are moving. To make students interested in sports, there is need for publicity and initiatives by schools and government institutions. Even the parents should consider the benefits of sports and encourage their children to participate in sports activities.

References:

1.	Adamu, B., Sani, M.U. and Abdu, A. (2006) Physical exercise and health: a review. Niger J. Med. 15(3): 190-196.
2.	Dodd, R., and Cassels, A. (2006) Centennial Review: Health Development and the Millennium Development Goals 100:5-6. Annals of Tropical Medicine & Parasitology at 379-387.
3.	Huber, M., Knottnerus, J.A., Green, L., Horst, H.V., Jadad, A.R., Kromhout, D., Leonard, B., Lorig, K., Loureiro, M.I., VanderMeer, J.W.M, Schnabel, P., Smith, R., VanWeel, C. and Smid, H. (2011) How should we define health? British Medical Journal. 343: 1-3
4.	Kelly, M. (2007) The Social Determinants of Health: Developing an Evidence Base for Political Action. Final Report to World Health Organization Commission on the

Social Determinants of Health (Measurement and Evidence Knowledge Network.

5. Rana, J.S., Li, T.Y. and Manson, J.E. (2007) Adiposity compared with physical inactivity and risk of type 2 diabetes in women. Diabetes Care. 30(1): 53-58.

6. WHO. Constitution of the World Health Organization. 2006. www.who.int/governance/eb/ who_constitution_en.pdf.

6

SOCIAL CONDITIONS OF WIDOWS IN INDIAN SOCIETY: A SOCIOLOGICAL ANALYSIS

Dr. Nav Shagan Deep Kaur [1]

Abstract

Widows had higher status in the Vedic period as the literature of the time reflects. During this period, numbers of widows were very small because of absence of early marriages. A young widow could marry if she wished, but in the post-vedic period, her position gave into subordination. Many people were against the widow remarriage. Discrimination and torture against widows increased during Mughal period. Sati became a status symbol and widow remarriage was prohibited. When Britishers came to India widow's condition was deplorable. The life of a Hindu widow was at its best one of incessant self- sacrifice and at its worst a record of unredeemed sorrows and sufferings, a long tale of troubles, hopelessness and helplessness. During this period social reformers tried to change the condition to some extent but this change was virtually transitory. In this Paper we discuss the social conditions of widows in Indian Society were analyzed.

Keywords: *widows, Indian Society, Women, Social.*

Introduction:

Widowhood is a universal phenomenon. It is a special case of mortality where the husband dies earlier than the wife. Sally cline, the author of the

---

[1] Assistant Professor, Department of Sociology, Sri Guru Granth Sahib World University, Fatehgarh Sahib. Punjab.

famous book, "lifiting the taboo; women, death and dying", observes: the old English word *'Widewe'* originated in the Indo-European root *"widh"* meaning to be empty or separated. The Sanskrit term a *"Vidh"* means a destitute or lacking. Joseph T. Shipley in the 'Dictionary of Word Origins' points out that, "Since marriage has made two of one, a widow is a woman that has been emptied of herself." Other writers confirm this notion: "She was a widow, that strange feminine entity who had once been endowed with a dual personality and was now only half of what she had been." (Cline:1997).

The New International Webster's Dictionary describes the word "widow" in the following three aspects:

1. A woman who has lost her husband by death, the female survivor of a marital union. A woman who has not remarried after the death of her husband. In the absence of express provision in the law with respect to the rights of a widow, her rights are not affected by a second marriage.

2. In the early church, one of special class of women, occupied as deaconesses in the works of charity and having some liturgical offices, as in the baptism of woman now found chiefly in designations of saints, as St. Monica, widow.

3. A woman deserted by her husband or without his company for a time; commonly qualified, as a gold widow.

Agarwal describes, widows, who in the earned tongue are called *'Vidhava'*, a word akin to the latin *'Vidua'* are given less respect than a *'sumangali'* and when they happen to have no children, they are generally looked upon with the utmost scorn. The very fact of meeting a widow is considered to bring ill luck (Agrawal: 1998).

Meera Khana observed that, once a widow, she is no longer the daughter-in-law, daughter or wife and is no individual anymore. The widow is socially dead entity. She is an observer, never an active participant in the society. As an observer, she is tolerated, but never welcomed.

Eraj Siddique, the author of the famous book, "*Women, Marriage and Family*", quoted Manu the first Hindu law giver. In the "Code of Manu" drawn up, woman's dependent position which was fully established in the sixth century B.C. to the third

A.D. In his words: "By a girl, by a young woman, or even by an aged one, nothing must be done independently, even in her own house. In childhood a female must be subject to her father, in youth to her husband, when her lord is dead to her sons; a woman must never be independent. She must not seek to separate herself from her father, husband or sons; by leaving them she would make both her own and her husband's families contemptible" (Siddique: 2005).

There are numerous texts prescribing the code of conduct for a widow and these have to a great extent formed the basis on which cultural pattern in society emerged. Interestingly these cultural patterns were uncompromisingly rigid for the higher castes than for the lower castes. Understandably, the higher castes to prove their superiority had to reiterate their rigid adherence to ritualistic Patterns .It is interesting also to note that the rigid standards were set out for those members of the caste who had no avenue of protest or rebellion.

Widows had higher status in the Vedic period as the literature of the time reflects. During this period, numbers of widows were very small because of absence of early marriages. A young widow could marry if she wished, but in the post-vedic period, her position gave into subordination. Many people were against the widow remarriage. Discrimination and torture against widows increased during Mughal period. Sati became a status symbol and widow remarriage was prohibited. When Britishers came to India widows condition was deplorable. The life of a Hindu widow was at its best one of incessant self- sacrifice and at its worst a record of unredeemed sorrows and sufferings, a long tale of troubles, hopelessness and helplessness. During this period social reformers tried to change the condition to some extent but this change was virtually transitory (Upadhyay: 2002).

Normally the status of women in Indian society has been

subordinate to men, right from the very beginning. They have undergone from various kinds of discriminations, exploitations and torture, both mental and physical in the society and within the four walls of the house. In the house which is supposed to be the safest place for its member's protection and development, the women are not only tortured, exploited and discriminated, but they are occasionally killed or burnt.

War can only bring death and destruction. By no means can it create happiness nor solve problems. History tells us that those who instigate war will eat their own evil fruits. Unfortunately India had to face three drastic attacks by her neighbor, Pakistan. In these three wars, no doubt, India, the great country has conducted herself admirably in bringing new international values into being. But at the same time, there is no denying that these wars have left thousands of women weeping and screaming whose husbands have sacrificed their lives in the defense of the country.

Thus to conclude the above discussion the social life style of widows which came out, shows that how much a woman is humiliated and tortured, just being a widow. The state of widowhood is not due to their own fault, but it is just a natural phenomenon. As it is well said that birth can be checked but death can't be. Any of the life partners can die anytime, but it is the woman only who is always blamed and has to undergo through various types of social, economic, physical and psychological harassments (Ranjan: 1989).

Widowhood is an issue which needs to be looked into from multidimensional perspectives. The present condition of the widows need to be considered from the social, economic and psychological points of view which are often indistinguishable from one another on account of a sharp contrast in the social attitude towards widows among the people of different socio-economic strata. Studies on widows carried out within an empirical framework are not many. There is a dearth of studies on widows in general and Kargil war widows in particular.

Traditionally, in Indian families widows were seen as liability. Indian society is more dynamic in religious superstitions and cultural practices where in a widow is deemed as a bad omen and forced to live a lonely, isolated and depressed life. In India, there is often an elaborated ceremony during the funeral of a widow's husband, which includes smashing the bangles, removing of the kumkum (bindi), colourful attire and widows are made to wear white clothes which are the indication of mourning. Traditionally in Indian society sati was a popular practice, where the widowed woman would throw herself on burning funeral pyre of her husband to immolate herself. A woman's existence was marked merely by her husband's physical presence. Widow remarriage was simply out of question.

The moment a woman becomes widow, she is deprived of average living conditions and benefits of worldly desires. A widow is considered as the second citizen in the society. The social stigma attached to the status of a widow is such that a widow has to burn herself 'day in' and 'day out' for years in the fire of social taboos, prejudices and social insult. When she is widowed in the husband's house she has nowhere to go. The truth is that the widow belongs to no one and has to find for herself against family, society and community at large. The presence of a widow was regarded as inauspicious on social occasions even in her own children's marriage.

Loneliness is one of another personal matter. There are several health hazards, psychological and physical trauma that a widow has to face. The grief and personal tragedy that they suffer as a consequence of widowhood is enormous. To fight it she had to forget the death of her husband but the customs, practices and society do exactly the reverse. They force upon the bereaved widow many external symbols of widowhood which day and night go on reminding her about her previous life and a great loss.

Our society highly out regard at the thought of cruelty. It was only unthinking cruelty that in rituals such as ceremonial breaking of wife's bangles upon the death of her husband, the forehead swept clean of the ones auspicious red *kumkum*, the colour discarded from the dress and a food code denied her all tasty and spicy food which was supposed to make her lustful. The widow had to take her food before sunset and observe all the religious fasts like *Ekadasi, Amavasya* etc. The most visible and traumatic of these rituals is the shaving of the hair on the head. This not only uglifies the widow, but also makes her realise her lessened power in the entire social order. A behaviour expected from her that she should not go out of the home. Even inside the home, she was not allowed to come out of her room or meet and speak to other family members especially males except minimally and when absolutely needed. She is expected to look dirty, unkept and smell foul. The more wretched and miserable she looks, the more she is respected. All this was supposed to be for her own protection so that she may not attract male attention. The belief is that the beauty of a woman is only for her husband and when a woman losses her husband she is supposed to look unattractive.

What horrifies human sensibilities is the humiliating manner in which these degrading practices are applied to a new widow. There is probably a vicarious pleasure in smearing the *Sindoor* and breaking the *Mangalsutra* violently. Women relatives used to break the bangles of the widow either with a stone or by hitting her hands against a wall. In some parts of India there was a practice that the *Sindoor* was wiped away with the toe of the dead husband's foot. In some parts of India widows had to drink the water in which the dead husband's body was washed. This is to prove the innocence of the widow that she is not responsible for the death of her husband in any way. All these practices widely followed by the higher castes in most parts of India till about three decades ago. Even today such practices still exist though not as widely prevalent as before. These evil practices were often imitated by the lower castes also with a view to emphasize their proximity to the higher castes.

Those widows who live perpetual misery carry the death of their husbands on their faces, are still glorified as paragons of virtual and ideal wives. As soon as a woman tries to forget her past and start living normal life, she is confronted with social criticism.

Society cannot tolerate her attempts to live a full meaningful life. Once the husband passes away, the wife left behind is literally left to face the hell. Finally a moral code prescribed that she should devote the rest of her life in prayer and observance of religious rituals involving fasting. Prayers were considered as the only way for her to atone for the sin of causing the death of her husband. All these practices have been in existence for so long, that no one has questioned or challenged them.

However, in modern culture the norms for clothing have gradually changed and given way to coloured clothing in a widow's life. Practice of sati has been banned in India for more than a century ago. The ban began under British rule and is much owed to the efforts of the social reformer, Raja Ram Mohan Roy, who asserted that sati was a means of showing status rather than a ritual in Indian society, and said that there are other ways of doing it than by burning the widows. Consequently, with this traditional mindset in India, entering into widowhood is more hazardous, humiliating and painful.

For centuries windows have been ill-treated, facing deprivation, poor economic status, lack of social support, poorhealth, denialof rights to food, clothing and shelter, discrimination in relation to work, dignity and participation in the community life. Their presence was considered unlucky and accursed. They were not allowed to join any auspicious occasion and they became the unpaid drudge.

This hard treatment has been greatly modified, but there are still many widows who are suffering much of the above described treatment. A widow has no place and status in the society. In the older days widow was a physical sati and now a days she is a psychological sati. While widowhood is always a trauma for a woman. India ranks highest in the world, in the incidence of widowhood. Every fourth household in India has a widow. Inspite of natural deaths, manmade factors like wars and terrorism increased the population of widows in the society. The impact of these wars is more on the women because more men are killed in these kinds of events and their wives are left without male support. But if it includes the above mentioned conditions and problems the life could become unbearable. Keeping this situation in the view the present study has been planned to assess the social, economic and psychological conditions of the widows.

References:

1. Aggarwal,Bina (1998); "*Widows versus Daughters: Property, Land And Economic Security in Rural India*"; Edited by Martha Alter Chen; Sage Publications, New Delhi.

2. Cline,Sally (1997); "*Lifting the Taboo; women, Death and Dying*"; NYU Press, New York.

3. Chakravarti,Uma (1993) ; "*Rewriting History: The life and times of Pandita Ramabai*"; The Women Press, Delhi.

4. Khana,Meera (2002); "*Trauma of Taboos and Tribulations of widowhood in India*"; Edited by V.Mohini

5. Giri; Gyan Publishing House, New Delhi.Kaur,manvinder and Sultana, Ameer (2009); "*Gender Realities*"; Abishek Publications, Chandigarh.

6. Moltke,Gen. (1993); "*Art of War*"; Presidio Press, New York.

7. Prasad,Dharmashila (1989); "*Sati' –In a Social Economic and Religious context*; Edited by Renu Rajan; Vikas Publishing House, Delhi.

8. Ranjan Renu (1989); "*Life-Style of Hindu Widows: An Expression of Violence Against Women*"; Vikas Publishing House, Delhi.

9. Sun,Tzu (2010); "*The Art of War*"; JAICO Publishing House, Mumbai.

10. Siddiqui,Eraj (2005); "*Women, Marriage and Family*"; Mark Publishers, Jaipur.

11. Sethi,Raj Mohini (2005); "*Living on The Edge: A Study of war Widows*"; Uppal Publishing House, Delhi

12. Upadhya,R.K. (2002); *"Widows in India : Today and Yesterday"*; Edited by V. Mohini Giri; Gyan Publishing House, New Delhi.

13. Witz,Gen.Carl V.C. (1970); *"On war"*; Princeton University Press, U.S.A.

7

OCCUPATIONAL STRESS AMONG TEACHERS TEACHING IN PRIVATE COLLEGES

Dr. Gurupreet Singh [1]

ABSTRACT

In the present study an attempt is made to study the occupational stress among teachers teaching in private colleges of Ludhiana district of Punjab. 100 teachers have been selected randomly from the various private colleges of Ludhiana district for the study. The occupational stress among the college teachers was measured by using the Occupational Stress Index given by Srivastava and Singh (1981). The independent samples t-test revealed that there was no significant difference between male and female teachers with respect to occupational stress and there was moderate occupational stress among teachers. Furthermore, there was significant (p<0.05) is occupational stress between permanent and ad-hoc teachers and the ad-hoc teachers experience greater occupational stress as compared to permanent teachers.

Keywords: *Stress, Occupational Stress, Private colleges, Teachers, Ad-hoc Teachers,*

INTRODUCTION

Stress in physics, is a force, which acts on a body to produce strain. Stress in psychophysiology is that stimulus which imposes detectable strain that cannot be

---

[1] Assistant Professor, Department of Physical Education, Malwa College Bondli, Samrala.

easily accommodated by the body and so presents itself as impaired health or behavior. Originally it had been derived from a Latin word 'stringere' meaning to 'draw tight'. In the 15th century the term stress was used as the shortened form of distress. In the beginning of the 20th century, the concept of stress appeared in medical literature and indicated the overloading of human body. According to International Dictionary of Education, "Stress is a state of anxiety, conflicts, heightened emotion and frustration, diagnosed from psychological and physiological symptoms". Stress is a universal phenomenon, excess of which result in intense and distressing experience. As a positive influence, stress can help to compel us to action; it can result in a new awareness and on exciting new perspective. While as a negative influence, it can result in feeling of distrust; rejection, anger and depression, which in turn can lead to health problems.

Occupational Stress

Stress related with job or occupation is called occupational stress. Occupational stress refers to a situation where occupation related factors interact with employee to change i.e. disrupts or enhance his/her psychological and physiological conditions such as the person is forced to deviate from normal functioning. He cannot work efficiently due to stress. An employee's job role, which is composed part of his job life and is responsible for bringing in maximum amount of job satisfaction or job stress, anxiety. Role of stress usually results from conflicting incompatible or unclear expectations that are derived from work environment.

Modern world is marked as world of stress that has become an established feature of human life now a day. The ever increasing needs and aspirations, tough competition, press use of meeting deadlines, uncertainty of future and weekend social support have made life at present diversely demanding and highly stressful.

The phenomenon of stress is not new rather people have experiencing it since the origin of structured societies. The causes of stress in those societies were episodic in nature and law in severity and frequency, hence were not a major threat to the lives of people. But during the last two of three decades, the multiplicity of causes, their frequency and severity have become a major threat to the well being of the people.

Review of Related Literature

Gupta (1980) revealed that the needs of achievement affiliation and endurance were positively related while needs of autonomy, dominance and aggression were negatively related to job satisfaction of primary school teachers. Secondary and college teachers almost equally satisfied with their job. Primary school teachers were significantly less satisfied than secondary teachers and college teachers. Beck and Srivatava (1991) compared the amount of stress experienced by in-service nursing teachers and student teachers and found that in-service teachers experienced more stress in comparison to student teachers. These findings have been discussed in terms of job conditions and the demands of occupation of in-service teachers. Gaur and Dhawan (2000) investigated the relationship between work related stress and adaptation pattern among women professionals and found that women in all the four professions i.e. teachers, bank officers and bureaucrats reported moderate work related stress. Kutty (2000) proposed reasons for stress at work place as work pressure, meeting deadline, positions in work place, interpersonal relationship, job content or profile, promotion and growth opportunities, imbalance between personal and professional commitments, consuming time especially from long distance suburban areas to the office. Deasthalee and Pravin (2000) found that age has no effect on the stress experienced by engineers. However the gender as well as education has displayed significant effect on job stress, male engineers experienced more than of females whereas the higher the education the lesser stress the engineers experienced. Jacobs and Schain (2009) conducted a study to find out the role stress of female professionals. They found that balancing domestic roles with a career imposes a serious stress on the professional females.

Lectures, doctors and administrators experience different type of stresses and to different degrees. Married female officers do not differ significant from unmarried officers on experimental role stress. Verma et al. (2002) explored burnout among primary school teachers in relation to gender, age and teaching experience (demographic variables). Results revealed that the level of burnout was almost similar among male and female teachers. Age was not related to burnout whereas the teaching experience was significantly and negatively correlated with the feeling of burn out. Recommendations have been made to reduce the feeling of burnout among primary school teachers. Marsall (2003) revealed that there was no significant difference found in occupational stress as measured by occupational role, adjustment.

Objectives of the Study

The objectives of the present study are

1. To study the occupational stress among teachers teaching in private colleges.
2. To investigate whether occupational stress is gender biased.
3. To study occupational stress among permanent and Ad-hoc teachers teaching in private colleges.

METHODOLOGY

The present study is entirely based upon primary cross section data, collected from 100 teachers of private colleges of Ludhiana district of Punjab. Out of these hundred teachers 50 are the male teachers and remaining 50 are the female teachers.

Tool Used for Data Collection

A well developed and widely used Occupational Stress Index (OSI) in the Indian context (Srivastava and Singh, 1981) was chosen to assess the occupational stress of the private college teachers. The questionnaire is consisted of 48 statements with five alternative responses e.g., 5 for strongly agree, 4 for mildly agree 3 agree, 2 for disagree and 1 for strongly disagree. Out of 46 items 28 are 'True -

Keyed' and last 18 are 'False — Keyed'. The items relate to almost all relevant components of the job size which cause stress in some way or the other, such as, role over-load, role ambiguity, role conflict, unreasonable group and political pressure, responsibility for persons, under participation, powerlessness, poor peer relations, intrinsic, impoverishment; low status, strenuous working conditions and unprofitability. Total score on this scale is considered for the assessment of occupational stress. More the score on this scale indicates more stress.

Statistical Analysis: Descriptive statistics such as mean and standard deviation were used to describe data. The independent samples t-test was utilized to assess the differences between the two groups. The significant levels was set at $p<0.05$. Data was analyzed using SPSS Version 16.0.

Table 1 Occupational stress among male and female teachers teaching in private colleges.

Group	N	Mean	SD	t-value	Result
Male Teachers	50	128.25	22.14		Insignificant at 0.05 level
Female Teachers	50	131.40	25.18	0.18	

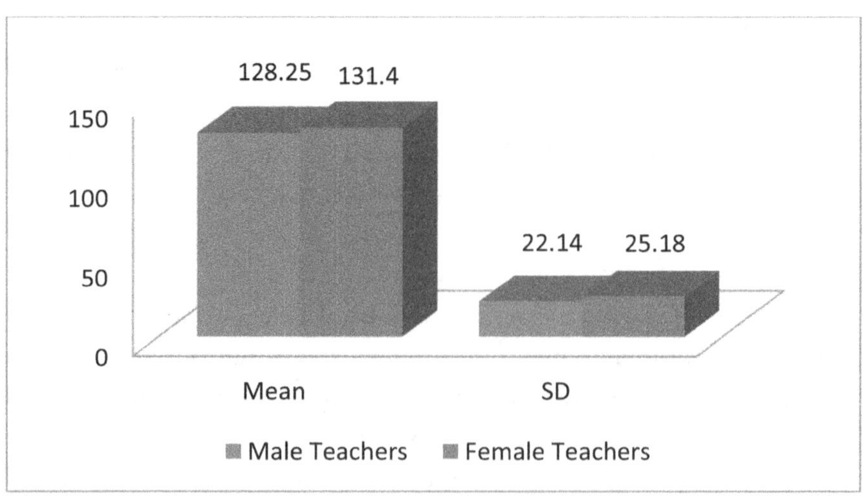

Table 2 Occupational stress among ad-hoc and permanent teachers teaching in private colleges.

Group	N	Mean	SD	t-value	Result
Ac-hoc Teachers	50	141.54	6.84	9.54	Insignificant at 0.05 level
Permanent Teachers	50	133.42	9.54		

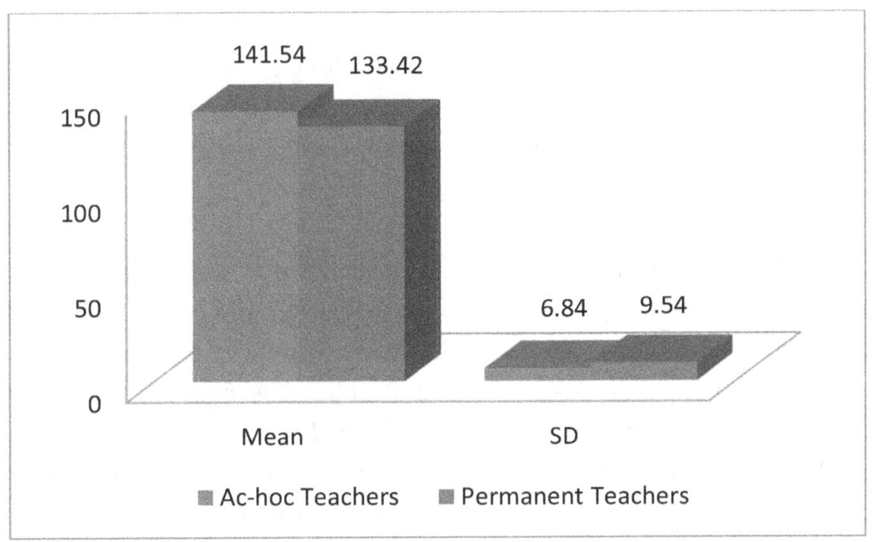

RESULTS

The results showed that means of teacher teaching in private colleges is 129.84 which fall in between 123-155 and according to the norm table this score stands for the moderate level of occupational stress among teachers in private colleges. The mean, standard deviation and t-value of male and female teachers teaching in private colleges with respect to occupational stress have been presented in table 1. The mean value of occupational stress of male teachers in private colleges was 128.88 and mean value of occupational stress of female teacher was 131.4. The standard deviations of male and female teachers were 22.18 and 25.18 respectively. Our calculated t value was 0.186 which was less than table value i.e. 2.06 at 0.05 levels which was insignificant. So there was no significant difference between male and female teachers with respect to occupational stress.

Further table 2 shows the mean, standard deviation and t-value of ad-hoc and permanent teachers teaching in private colleges with respect to occupational stress. The mean values of occupational stress of ad-hoc teachers in private colleges was 141.54 and mean value of occupational stress of permanent teachers was 133.42. Standard deviations of ad-hoc and permanent teachers were 6.84 and 9.80 respectively. Our calculated 't' value was 9.54 which was greater than table value of 2.06 at 0.05 level, which was significant. Thus there was significant difference in the occupational stress of the ad-hoc and permanent teachers in private colleges.

Discussion

The main objectives of the present study were to identify the stress levels in private college teachers, and to examine the differences in stress levels on the basis of gender and nature of job (i.e. permanent vs ad-hoc teachers). The present study has shown that, in line with other studies elsewhere (e.g. Zakiah, 2003; Dussault et al., 1997), the overall stress levels among teachers is moderate. The results reveal no gender differences in stress levels, which mean that male and female college teachers appear to have the same levels of stress. These results are consistent with the findings of Abouserie (1996), Tuettemann and Punch (1990) and Zakiah (2003), but not with those of Dussault et al. (1997), Kyriacou and Sutcliffe (1978), and Borg et al. (1991). The present study also indicated that there was significant difference between ad-hoc and permanent teachers of private colleges and the ad-hoc teachers experience higher levels of occupational stress. The basic reason for the significant difference can be attributed to the fact that permanent teachers in private colleges have more job security, less accountability, less workload, and also have provision for other facilities like promotions, medical facilities and even more provision of leaves and holidays in comparison to ad-hoc teachers in private colleges. Ad-hoc teachers are held more accountable, have less job security and less provision of other facilities.

Conclusion

The present investigation is an attempt to study the occupational stress among teachers teaching in private colleges. It is concluded in the study that there was no significant difference between the male and female teachers teaching in private colleges. On the other hand, there was significant difference between ad-hoc and permanent teachers with respect to occupational stress.

REFERENCES

1. Abouserie R. (1996). Stress, coping strategies, and job satisfaction in university academic staff *Educational Psychology*, 16, 49-56.

2. Beck DL, Srivastava, R. (1991). Perceived level and sources of stress in baccalaureate nursing students. *Journal of Nursing Education*, 30(3), 127- 133.

3. Borg MG, Riding RJ, Faizon 3M. (1991). Stress in Teaching: A Study of Occupational Stress. and Its Determinants, Job Satisfaction and Career Commitment Among Primary Schoolteachers. *Educational Psychology*, 11 (1): 5 -75.

4. Deostnalee, Pravin G. (2000). A study of effect of gender, age and educational maturity on job stress. *Psycho-Lingura*, 30 (1):57-60.

5. Dussault M, Deaudelin C, Royer N, Loiselle J. (1997). Professional isolation and stress in teachers. Paper presented at the American Education Research Association, Chicago, IL.

6. Gaur SP, Dhawan N. (2000). Work related stressors and adaptation pattern among women professionals. *Psychological Studies*, 45(1&2): 58-63.

7. Gupta SP. (1980). A study of job satisfaction at three levels of teaching. Buch, M.B.1987, ed., Third Survey of Research in Education, NCERT, New Delhi, 809-810.

8. Jacobs P, Schain L. (2009). Professional women: The continue struggle acceptance and equality. *Journal of Academic and Business ethics*, 1:98-111.

9. Kutty S. (2000). Managing stress, anticipate, apprehend asses and planned well get rid of stress "I-lead Start" The' Indian express 01. Issue (24) Managing stress.

10. Kyriacou C, Sutcliffe J. (1978). Teacher Stress: Prevalence, Sources and Symptoms. *British Journal of Educational Psychology*, 48: 159-167.

11. Marshall VG. (2003). Occupational Stress of International Society for performance improvement member. *Dissertation Abstracts International*, 63(7), 2617.

12. Srivastava AK, Singh AP. (1981). Manual of the Occupational stress Index, Department of Psychology, Barnaras University, Varanasi.

13. Tuettemann E, Punch KF. (1990). Stress levels among secondary school teachers. *Educational Review*, 42 (1), 25-29.

14. Verma S, Kadhari, Sharma N. (2002). A study of occupational stress Cmel Mental Health among defence personal. *Indian Psychological Abstracts and Reviews*, 10, pp.122.

15. Zakiah Binti Arshad. (2003). Stress Kerja di Kalangan Guru-guru Sekolah Rendah: Satu Kajian di Zon Bandar, Kota Tinggi, Johor. University Teknologi Malaysia: Tesis Sarnaja.

8

EFFECT OF MENTAL IMAGERY TRAINING ON GOAL SCORING DURING PENALTY KICK OF SOCCER FEMALE PLAYERS

Atinder Bikramjit Singh Mal [1]

ABSTRACT

This study was determined to identify the effects of Mental Imagery Training on goal scoring of the penalty kicks by a soccer female player. A total of 60 female soccer players from Madhya Pradesh, whose average of scoring goal during penalty kick ranges from 0-3 out of 10 penalty kicks in 2 trials were selected. The subjects were further randomly divided into two groups namely MIT (Mental Imagery Training Group) N = 30 and CG (Control Group) N = 50. Both the groups did regular soccer training; followed by 20 minutes of mental imagery training (by MIT Group only) for 5 days in a week and for 6 weeks respectively, while Control group received the soccer training session only. The results of the study showed that both the groups had significantly improved in the rate of goal scoring in the penalty kick as the value obtained for MIT & CG was found 10.725 at p= 0.05 respectively. Levene's Test of Equality of Error Variances showed that data were normally distributed. The pairwise analysis confirms that the percentage improvement differs significantly between the groups as the mean differences obtained for CG- MIT is 1.164 at p= 0.05. Therefore it was concluded that mental imagery training was proved to be effective means for the improvement in goal scoring in penalty kick of soccer and hence it

[1] Assistant Professor, Department of Physical Education, Sri Guru Granth Sahib World University, Fatehgarh Sahib.

may be used as an part of cognitive training for the making an soccer player.

***Index Terms**- Mental Imagery Training, Penalty kick, soccer.*

INTRODUCTION

In recent years the study of mental imagery has sparked the interest of many scholars in the field of sport psychology. It is now recognized that, in general, imagery is used daily by most people (Barr & Hall, 1992). In addition, many athletes and coaches have realized the important role that imagery plays (Salmon, Hall, &Haslam, 1994) and have incorporated its use in into their training regimens (Martin, Moritz, & Hall, 1999).

Mental imagery can be defined as the process that occurs when we recreate experiences in the mind using information that is stored in the memory. Dreaming is an unstructured form of imagery, but the type of imagery we're interested in here is structured imagery, where the athlete uses his or her imagination in a controlled fashion to recreate specific images. There are a number of different ways of visualizing images or experiences recreated in the mind (e.g. you can visualize yourself feeling movement internally, or externally as a spectator) but research shows that the more able an athlete is to control his or her imagined movements, the greater the potential performance enhancement (Advances in Sport Psychology (2nd ed), Champaign IL: Human Kinetics, 2002:405-439)

These aspects of the mental imagery process needs to be constantly practice in order to elicit results. Even though individual differences exist in mental imagery ability, generally, better imagery control correlates to better performance in the motor skill (Annett, 1995).

Objectives And Hypothesis

The study was conducted with the objectives to determine the effect of Mental Imagery Training on goal scoring on penalty kick in soccer. After thoroughly going through the literature it was hypothesized that there would be significant effect of Mental Imagery Training on goal scoring of the penalty kick conversion in soccer.

Experimental Design

Pre-test and post test randomized group design was employed in the study. The subjects were divided into experimental group and control group. The experimental group was imparted 20 minutes of training of mental imagery for six weeks under the supervision and guidance of the scholar. While no training was imparted to control group. At the end of six weeks post test was conducted for both the group.

PROCEDURE AND METHODOLOGY

The study was conducted on 60 female soccer players from Madhya Pradesh, whose average of goal scoring in the penalty kick ranges from 0-3 out of 10 penalty strokes in 2 trials. The selected subjects were further randomly divided into two groups namely MIT (Mental Imagery Training Group) N = 30, and CG (Control Group) N = 30. Both the groups did regular soccer training; followed by 20 minutes of mental imagery training (by MIT Group only) for 5 days in a week and for 6 weeks respectively, while Control group received the soccer training session only. Throughout the test, penalty kicks were taken alternately by two penalty kicks specialists (N=2) i.e. 5 kicks by each player. ($2\times5=10$). Standard penalty kicks procedure was used as the criterion measure. Both the groups did soccer training for 5 days a week and for 6 weeks, while the MIT group did an extra 20 minutes session of Mental Imagery Training respectively.

To study the effect of MIT on goal scoring of Penalty Kicks in soccer descriptive statistics (Mean & SD) were employed. While ANCOVA was used to determine the significant difference between the groups.

Statistical Technique:

In order to find out the effect of mental imagery training ANCOVA was calculated. The level of significance was set at 0.05.

RESULTS:

Table 1:-Descriptive Statistics

Dependent Variable: post

treatment	Mean	Std. Deviation	N
experimental group	3.0667	1.50707	30
control group	1.8333	1.31525	30
Total	2.4500	1.53408	60

Table 2:-Tests of Between-Subjects Effects

Dependent Variable: post

Source	Type I Sum of Squares	Df	Mean Square	F	Sig.	Noncent. Parameter	Observed Powerb
Corrected Model	31.657a	2	15.828	8.417	.001	16.834	.956
Intercept	360.150	1	360.150	191.510	.000	191.510	1.000
Pre	11.487	1	11.487	6.108	.016	6.108	.681
Treatment	20.170	1	20.170	10.725	.002	10.725	.896
Error	107.193	57	1.881				
Total	499.000	60					
Corrected Total	138.850	59					

a. R Squared = .228 (Adjusted R Squared = .201)

b. Computed using alpha = .05

Table 3:-Pairwise comparison

(I) treatment	(J) treatment	Mean Difference (I-J)	Std. Error	Sig.b	95% Confidence Interval for Differenceb	
					Lower Bound	Upper Bound
experimental group	control group	1.164*	.356	.002	.452	1.876
control group	experimental group	-1.164*	.356	.002	-1.876	-.452

Based on estimated marginal means

*. The mean difference is significant at the .05 level.

b. Adjustment for multiple comparisons: Least Significant Difference (equivalent to no adjustments).

Discussion & Findings

Table- 3 clearly reveals the pairwise comparison of the post scores of goal scoring in penalty kick of soccer showing that both the two groups were significantly differs after receiving the mental imagery training. As the mean difference is .002 which is less than .05

Conclusion

The study concludes that cognitive trainings like mental imagery training is very effective for goal scoring of the penalty kick in soccer and hence it can prove to be a use full training aspect for the making of a soccer player.

REFERENCES

1.　Shanahan Richard, Hyland.M.UU John, DBS, (2011). The Use of Mental Imagery Techniques to Improve Free Kick Accuracy in GAA Footballers, The Irish Psychologist.

2.　Hegazy Khaled, Sherif Mohamed Amin, Houta Shapan Samir (2015), The effect of Mental Training on Motor Performance of Tennis and Field Hockey Strokes in Novice Players

3.　Routhan Tarun, Jaggi Singh Devender, Negi Gaurav (2014), Effect of Mental Imagery Training & Tratak Kriya on Stopping of Penalty Strokes in Hockey, International Journal of Scientific and Research Publications, ISSN 2250-3153

4.　Hinshaw E. Karin (1970), The Effects of Mental Practice on Motor Skill Performance: Critical Evaluation and Meta-Analysis, Imagination Cognition and Personality

5.　Surburg R.Paul, Porretta L.David, Sutlive Vins (1995), Use of Imagery Practice for Improving a Motor Skill, Human Kinetics Publishers,Inc. 12, 217-227.

6.　Reddy Venkata Bora, Valli Shilpa Karanam (2014), Effect of Meditational Practices on Movement Time, Reaction Time, Anxiety and Perception Among Elite Atheletes of Andhra Pradesh, International Journal of Health, Physical Education and Computer Science in Sports, 15, 71-72.

7.   Pavio, (1985). Cognitive and Motivational Functions of Imagery in Human Performance, Journal of Applied Sports Science, 10, 22-28

9

IMPORTANCE AND INFLUENCE OF SELF CONFIDENCE IN SPORTS ACHIEVEMENT

Dr Paramjit Kaur [1]

Introduction:

Self-confidence is how firmly athletes believe in their ability to execute a physical skill or perform a task. Confidence is derived from a baseline assessment of past performances, training, and preparation. Confidence is a cure-all for what ails athletes' mental game. If athletes have high self-confidence, it's very hard to get anxious or tense, or worry about results because they already know that they will perform well. With high confidence, they don't fret about the competition. Self-confidence is an attitude about your skills and abilities. It means you admit and trust yourself and have a sense of control in your life. You are well aware of your strengths and weakness well, and have a optimistic view of yourself. You set realistic expectations and goals, converse assertively, and can handle disapproval.

On the contrary low self-confidence makes a person feel full of self-doubt, the person may be passive or submissive, or have difficulty trusting others. These people may also feel inferior, unloved and are sensitive to criticism. Feeling confident might also depend on the situation. For instance, a person can feel very confident in some areas, such as academics, but lack confidence in others, like relationships. Having high or low self-confidence is rarely related to the actual abilities of a person and is mostly based on your perceptions. Perceptions are the way people think about

---

[1] Assistant Professor, GHG Khalsa College, Gurusar Sadhar (Ldh.)

themselves. Low self-confidence can stem from different experiences, such as growing up in an unsupportive and critical environment, being separated from friends or family for the first time, judging one's own self too harshly, or being afraid of failure. People with low self-confidence often have errors in their thinking. Confidence is the most important aspect of a person's performance in various areas and in sports performance as well.

Self Confidence and Achievement Behaviours: Confidence has also been linked to productive achievement behaviours such as increased effort and persistence. In their processing efficiency theory, Eysenck and Calvo (1992) argued that a decrease in performance efficiency as a result of anxiety might manifest itself in higher subjective effort, but only if participants felt they had a reasonable chance of success. Furthermore, a strong sense of confidence has been associated with the setting of challenging goals and the expenditure of maximal effort and persistence to achieve those goals (Bandura, 1986). Thus, athletes who are high in confidence are likely to succeed because of their productive achievement behaviours. In addition to goal attainment, the attributions made by individuals to appraise success and failure have been found to influence expectations and motivation for future.

Confidence has been consistently associated with positive affect, whereas a lack of confidence has been associated with anxiety, depression, and dissatisfaction (e.g. Martens, Vealey, & Burton, 1990; Vealey, 1986; Vealey & Campbell, 1988; Vealey, Hayashi, Garner-Holman, & Giacobbi, 1998). Recent investigations within the stress domain have found self-confidence to be a moderating factor in the interpretation of pre-competition symptoms, where high confidence in some way protects or overrides debilitative interpretations of pre-competition emotions usually perceived as negative i.e. anxiety (Mellalieu, Neil & Hanton, 2006). These propositions seem to accord with anecdotal reports of athletes performing exceptionally well when they are feeling both anxious and self-confident.

The conceptualization of sport confidence as specific and unique to sport was intended to enhance understanding in the field of sport psychology (Vealey, 1986). However, despite Vealey's (2001) proposals that sport confidence influences performance through its affect on how athletes think about, feel about, and respond to everything that happens to them in sport, the processes and mechanisms that underlie confidence have been largely ignored.

One of the most consistent findings in the peak performance literature is the significant correlation between self-confidence and successful sporting performance (Feltz, 2007). Thus, it is perhaps not surprising that the study of self-confidence has featured prominently in sport psychology literature, with social cognitive theories such as Bandura's (1977) self-efficacy theory provides the basis for most of this work.

Hays and colleagues (Hays, Maynard, Thomas & Bawden, 2007) were the first to investigate sport confidence in successful world-class sports performers. They identified sources and types of confidence used by athletes competing on the world stage and demonstrated that demographic and organizational factors influence the development of confidence in such athletes. It was found that women athletes derived confidence from a perceived competitive advantage, such as seeing their competitors perform badly, or crack under the pressure of competition and men just believed they were better than their competitors. It was also suggested that female world-class athletes tend to be situationally dependent on external information in establishing performance expectations.

Athletes who derive their confidence from uncontrollable sources could develop weaker or unstable perceptions of control and competence. Corbin (1981) found that the threat of playing "a good opponent" could create a vulnerability in women that is not experienced by men. Consequently, with regard to perceptions of sport confidence, female world-class athletes might be more susceptible to factors associated with the organizational culture of world-class sports performance. Previously, researchers have demonstrated that while male athletes generally demonstrate greater confidence than female athletes they are also less susceptible to changes in self-confidence during the pre-competition period .

Steps to boost confidence and performance of players

During competitions sportspersons may feel nervous, unsettled, or feel more pressure to play their best. Young athletes may experience excitement or nervous jitters before and during competition. Athletes who feel jitters are the players who may under perform. Some young athletes may have a fear of embarrassment or fear of making mistakes. Some athletes make comparisons with other athletes, which is not always healthy for kids' confidence. Some players may be worried about impressing a coach or parent. Some athletes are held back because they lack confidence and have doubts. Other athletes may try to perform perfectly and tie themselves up in knots doing so .At the time of competitions the following tips can be use as a measure to deal with confidence issues.

Coping with Panic:

In sports, most of the fear athletes experience to is not about being in danger or harming themselves physically, although in some sports like hockey, players can be physically injured. The fear is about a psychological threat that is often based on an athlete's perception of the importance of a performance or game and what others think about his or her performance.

Most of the time, an athlete's fear is worry related to poor results – whether prior to or during a performance. Athletes often fear the negative consequences of their performance. They worry about many things that are often not under their control.

The very first step is to identify the beliefs, attitudes, and expectations that cause your athletes to hold onto over-exactness in competition and lead to fear of failure. You want your athletes to keep the positive aspects of their mental game such as your motivation and commitment to sport. However, maintaining beliefs or attitudes that support a fearful, cautious, or over-seriousness attitude when performing does not allow kids perform their best. Thoughts such as "I must be perfect if I want to make the team today" or "I must analyse my mistakes and fix them right away so I don't make the same mistake" cause players to play tentatively.

Mental Toughness:

During mental toughness training, I teach my students about two mindsets that contribute to success in sports. The first is the training or practice mindset. Great athletes know the value of training. They strive to get better and to improve. They have a tremendous amount of motivation and work ethic, which help them to practice hard so they can master their skills. The trusting or performance mindset is equally important for success in sports. Trust is the ability to let skills "happen" instinctively by relying on practice instead of consciously directing movements. The performance mindset is the ability to rely on practice, perform freely, and allow skills to flow without excess thought. If the athletes are stuck in the practice mentality when they compete, they will limit their ability to perform their best because of too much analysis, trying too hard to be perfect, and a loss of trust.

Self Intimidation:

Your athletes must start with the understanding that most intimidation in sports is self-induced. Yes, other athletes will sometimes use direct intimidation or play head games with your athletes, but they can make the choice to not pay attention and look the other way. However, the athletes can't "look the other way" when they are their own worst enemy because they are intimidated by their own thoughts about the level of the competition, the rink conditions, or the venue. Athletes who lack confidence often look for others to help them feel confident. Likewise, these same athletes intimidate themselves by paying too much attention to other hockey players or by putting other hockey players on a pedestal.Most self-induced intimidation comes from your athletes giving too much energy to other competitors by making comparisons, thinking too much about the reputation of their competitors, or feeling like they do not belong at the current level of play.

Self-Intimidation can be overcome by the following methods:

- The athlete should avoid thinking about other athletes.
- The athlete should stop making comparisons to athletes who they think are better.
- Athletes can focus on their strengths instead thinking about the reputation of other competitors and how they stack up.
- Athletes should be helped to see themselves on equal ground in terms of their ability.

Social Approval:

Social approval is an important phenomenon in my discussions with athletes that I coach. Many athletes rely too much on social approval to boost their own levels of self-worth. Some athletes think that if others respect their sports performance, this, for some reason, will make them a better person. Many athletes buy into this notion and think that they are better people if they can achieve acknowledgment, gain approval or respect from others through sports.

For many athletes, a huge source of worry about their performance results from the need to seek "social approval" from others. If this is your athlete, they might have a need to be admired, accepted, respected, or liked by other people. They worry about performing poorly because it may have an influence on what others might think about them.

Thus, athletes who want approval from others can become anxious or are afraid to fail in competition. The need for social approval is the root of fear of failure. But this story gets even better. What happens when your athletes want approval, but can't get it? Does this affect how they feel about themselves as people? For most of my students, yes! Athletes want approval from others so they can feel better about themselves!

Tips to Stop Worrying What Others Think

- Athletes should try to understand why they value others' opinions. Help your athletes stop the mind reading or thinking too much about what others might think.
- Athletes can learn to separate self-esteem and performance. Most of the athletes judge themselves on their performance in sports.

Functional Mindset:

An important lesson I teach my students is to learn how to perform efficiently instead of perfectly. I call this a "functional mindset." A functional mindset is the opposite of trying to make everything perfect. It starts with the idea that your athletes DO NOT have to be perfect to perform their best. They are human and humans can't be perfect. Your athletes will make mistakes and you and your athletes have to accept mistakes. Tennis coach to professional players, Brad Gilbert, calls the functional mindset "winning ugly," which he wrote a book about. Athletes can play functionally with the help of the following tips:

- Athletes should warm up to get a "feel" for their performance. They should remember not to judge the quality of their technique or performance in the warm up.
- Athletes should let go of the need to control their performance and let it happen.
- The coaches should use whatever works to help them get the job done in tryouts. For example, instead of needing to execute a play exactly from the playbook, be happy with a play that worked well, but maybe was not "textbook" execution.

Doubt is the number one killer to a confident mindset. Pessimistic, perfectionistic and over-motivated athletes tend to hold on tight to doubts, which if unchecked can ruin an athlete's mindset and derail performance. Some athletes start doubting before they even start the competition or make an error. Most athletes struggle with doubt after making a mistake or performing poorly in competition. When they let doubt run rampant and unchecked, it sabotages confidence.

Focus Only On Performance :

Athletes have the unique ability to selectively attend to what they want. This mental skill comes in handy when they perform, but only if they focus on the right performance cues. A performance cue is any thought, feeling, or image that helps you execute. A hockey player might feel his wrist flick on the shot. Understanding what is not relevant is an important step in helping your athletes improve focus by understanding their distraction. Many of the athletes tend to overload their brains with too much information – more than they can handle at one time. Information overload or having misleading information sends mixed signals to the body. In this indecisive state, the body will not execute with the desired outcome or rhythm. Learning any new skill takes time.

Injury and illness: Athletes identified injury or illness as a factor responsible for debilitating their feelings of sport confidence going into an important competition. These athletes described a reduced confidence in their physical ability to perform, which ultimately affected their performance. As one World Cup winner highlighted: "It was not the lack of confidence in my own ability, it was the lack of confidence in my ankle performing to the level that I needed it to in the game situation ... So if I was going into contact I'd go in a bit slower, or I'd try and get into a position where I knew that my ankle was going to be alright, and I'd do a job but not at the standard that it needed to be".

Poor preparation:

Athletes also identified poor preparation as a factor responsible for reduced feelings of sport confidence. Their reactions pertain largely to poor physical training, or not doing enough in training and consequently feeling underprepared. One female World Champion highlighted: "There've been times where I know that I'm on a roll therefore I know I'm going to win the championship. But there have also been times when I've gone in there not fully fit or fully prepared, I haven't done enough, and therefore you're at a 5–10% disadvantage straight away because you're thinking that in your head".

Coaching:

Athletes also identified factors relating to coaching as debilitative to their confidence. One athlete spoke about a coach who had been detrimental to her self-confidence by calling her "fat". This athlete explained how her coach "knocked every insecurity I had and kept knocking me down thinking that he'd make me tough and he didn't". Additional factors identified as debilitative to sport confidence included spending less time with a personal coach.

Pressure and expectations:

The pressure and expectations associated with successful performance were also identified as being debilitative to sport confidence. Self-doubt as a consequence of high expectations is a common theme among the athletes and was related to qualifying for major championships in addition to championship outcomes. Thus, reaching the pinnacle of their sporting career actually seemed to reduce the athletes' sport confidence. In contrast, the pressure and expectations associated with world-class competition did not seem to affect the males' feelings of sport confidence. Rather, expectations seemed to motivate these athletes to succeed. Factors responsible for debilitating sport confidence

Research has also identified sources and types of confidence used by athletes competing on the world stage and demonstrated that demographic and organizational factors influence the development of confidence in such athletes. For example, women athletes derived confidence from a perceived competitive advantage, such as seeing their competitors perform badly, or crack under the pressure of competition. In contrast, men just believed they were better than their competitors. Lirgg, George, Chase, &

Ferguson (1996) suggest that world-class athletes tend to be situationally dependent on external information in establishing performance expectations.

Conclusion:

The role of confidence in relation to the cognitive, affective, and behavioural responses in sports persons has been examined and factors responsible for fluctuating confidence have also been identified. In support of research that has demonstrated a positive correlation between high sport confidence and successful sporting performance, it was found that the athletes performed successfully when their feelings of sport confidence were high, and unsuccessfully when they were experiencing low sport confidence. On examination of the processes and perceived mechanisms underlying confidence effects, high sport confidence was found to be synonymous with positive affect, effective competition behaviours, and effective competition focus. In contrast, low sport confidence was identical with negative affect, ineffective competition behaviours, and an inability to maintain an effective competition focus.

References

1.   Bandura, A. 1977. Self-efficacy: Toward a unifying theory of behaviour change. Psychological Review, 84: 191–215.
2.   Bandura, A. 1986. Social foundations of thought and action, Englewood Cliffs, NJ: Prentice-Hall.
3.   Corbin, C. B. 1981. Sex of subject, sex of opponent and opponent ability as factors affecting self-confidence in a competitive situation. Journal of Sport Psychology, 4: 265–270. [Google Scholar]
4.   Cresswell, S. and Hodge, K. 2004. Coping skills: Role of trait sport confidence and trait anxiety. Perceptual and Motor Skills, 98: 433–438. [Web of Science], [Google Scholar]

5. Eysenck, M. W. and Calvo, M. G. 1992. Anxiety and performance: The processing efficiency theory. Cognition and Emotion, 6: 409–434 [Google Scholar]

6. Feltz, D. L. 2007. "Self-confidence and sports performance". In Essential readings in sport and exercise psychology, Edited by: Smith, D. and Bar-Eli, M. 278–294. Champaign, IL: Human Kinetics.

7. Gernigon, C. and Delloye, J. B. 2003. Self-efficacy, causal attribution, and track athletic performance following unexpected success or failure among elite sprinters. The Sport Psychologist, 17: 55–76.

8. Gill, D. L. 2000. Psychological dynamics of sport and exercise, 2nd edn., 255–268. Champaign, IL: Human Kinetics. [Google Scholar]

9. Hanton, S. and Connaughton, D. 2002. Perceived control of anxiety and its relationship to self-confidence and performance. Research Quarterly for Exercise and Sport, 73: 87–98. [Google Scholar]

10. Hays, K., Maynard, I., Thomas, O. and Bawden, M. 2007. So urces and types of confidence identified by World Class sport performers. Journal of Applied Sport Psychology, 19: 434–456. [Taylor & Francis Online], [Web of Science ®], [Google Scholar]

11. Jones, G. and Hanton, S. 2001. Pre-competitive feeling states and directional anxiety interpretations. Journal of Sports Sciences, 19: 385–395. [Taylor & Francis Online], [Google Scholar]

12. Kane, M. J. 1989. The post Title IX female athlete in the media. Journal of Physical Education, Recreation, and Dance, 60: 58–62. [Taylor & Francis Online], [Google Scholar]

13. Kane, M. J. and Parks, J. B. 1992. The social construction of gender difference and hierarchy in sport journalism – few new twists on very old themes. Women in Sport and Physical Activity Journal, 1: 49–83. [Google Scholar]

14. Lirgg, C. D. 1991. Gender differences in self-confidence in physical activity: A meta analysis of recent studies. Journal of Sport and Exercise Psychology, 13: 294–310. [Google Scholar]

15. Lirgg, C. D., George, T. R., Chase, M. A. and Ferguson, R. H. 1996. Impact of conception of ability and sex-type of task on male and female self-efficacy. Journal of Sport and Exercise Psychology, 18: 426–434. [Google Scholar]

16. Martens, R., Vealey, R. S. and Burton, D. 1990. Competitive anxiety in sport, Champaign, IL: Human Kinetics.

17. Mellalieu, S.D., Neil, R. and Hanton, S. 2006. An investigation of the mediating effects of self-confidence between anxiety intensity and direction. Research Quarterly for Sport and Exercise, 77: 263–270. [Taylor & Francis Online]

18. Thomas, O., Hanton, S. and Maynard, I. 2007. Anxiety responses and psychological skill use during the time leading up to competition: Theory to practice I. Journal of Applied Sport Psychology, 19: 379–398. [Google Scholar]

19. Vealey, R. S. 1986. Conceptualization of sport-confidence and competitive orientation: Preliminary investigation and instrument development. Journal of Sport Psychology, 8: 221–246.

20. Vealey, R. S. 1988. Sport-confidence and competitive orientation: An addendum on scoring procedures and gender differences. Journal of Sport and Exercise Psychology, 10: 471–478.

21. Vealey, R. S. 2001. "Understanding and enhancing self-confidence in athletes". In Handbook of sport psychology, Edited by: Singer, R. N., Hausenblas, H. A. and Janelle, C. M. 550–565. New York: Wiley.

22. Vealey, R. S. and Campbell, J. L. 1988. Achievement goals of adolescent figure skaters: Impact of self-confidence, anxiety and performance. Journal of Adolescent Research, 3: 227–243.

10

AN ANAYLATICAL STUDY OF PERCEPTION AS RELATED TO GENDER AND PERFORMANCE OF PANJAB UNIVERSITY FOOTBALLERS

Dr. Baljinder Singh [1]

ABSTRACT

Purpose of Study: The purpose of the present study was to investigate the perception variations of winner and looser football groups among male and female football players. **Method:** For the purpose of the present study, teams securing first, second, third and fourth place in Panjab University Inter College (male) and Panjab University Inter college (female) football tournaments and teams (both male and female) who lost in the first round were selected as sample. For collection of data, *SIZE WEIGHT ILLUSION PERCEPTION TEST* constructed by Postman, Bruner and Mc Ginnies (1948) was used to measure perception of the subjects. After statistical analysis, the value of mean and standard deviation of the perception variable was computed and 't' test was applied to find out the significance of difference between the scores of winners and losers on perception variable. The study was tested at .05 level of significance. **Finding**: The study revealed that winner group among winner- looser category and male group among male-female category was better than other group on perception variable.

Key words: *perception, football, winners and losers*

---

[1] Assistant Professor, GHG Khalsa College Gurusar Sadhar (Ludhiana)

INTRODUCTION

Football is most popular sporting event throughout world. It is played by 250 million players in over 200 countries, making it the world's most popular sport. The game is played on a rectangular field with a goal at each end. The object of the game is to score by using any part of the body besides the arms and hands to get the football into the opposing goal. There is hardly a corner on the earth where people of all ages and both sex have not attracted by this game, amazing accuracy and sometimes thrilling extra ordinary finishes. Football game is a combination of masterful skills, aesthetic body movements and psychological setup. The experts in the field believe that marked changes and advancement in the game's technique and tactics as well as multivariate strategies is the outcome of scientific as well as psychological approach.

Indian standard of football is very low as compared to European & Latin American countries. India's performance against these countries is like a small baby competing against a big giant. One of the reasons why we are lacking behind may be lack of adequate research on different aspects related to playing ability in football & psychological training in various situations.

Although many studies have looked at the perceptual-cognitive strategies used to make anticipatory judgments in sport, few have examined the informational invariants that our visual system may be attuned to. Using immersive interactive virtual reality to simulate the aerodynamics of the trajectory of a ball with and without sidespin, the present study examined the ability of Panjab University football players to make judgments about the ball's future arrival position. An analysis of their perception shows that subjects were strongly influenced by the ball's positions. The changes in ball position caused by sidespin led to erroneous predictions about the ball's future arrival position. Perception analysis plays a vital role to enhance football skills.

Keeping in mind the above mentioned factors, we come to the conclusion that proper knowledge of psychology and its implementations are needed at every step in football training and coaching to the footballers to attain maximum performance. The researcher thus undertakes the study on perception variations of winner and looser football groups among male and female football players of Panjab University Chandigarh.

OBJECTIVES OF THE STUDY

The present study has the following objectives.

1. To find out significant differences between total sample of winner and loser football players on the variable perception.
2. To find out significant differences between total sample of male and female football players on the variable perception.

PROCEDURE AND METHODOLOGY

This was a survey study which focuses to assess the psychological variable i.e. perception of Panjab University Intercollege football players. The purposive sampling technique were used to select the subjects for the study. The players of first four position holding teams in Panjab University Intercollege(male) Panjab University Intercollege (female) were considered as winners and the players of the teams losing in the first round were considered as losers for the collection of data in both gender groups i.e. (male and female)

To measure size weight illusion of the subjects *SIZE WEIGHT ILLUSION PERCEPTION TEST* constructed/developed by Postman, Bruner and Mc Ginnies (1948) and modified by Arguin, Marlin and Patrick (1988) was administered.

The test consists of trying to match the weight of 10 cylinders with respect to a standard cylinder of 70gms which is one third the height of the test cylinders. The diameter remaining same the test cylinders vary in increments of 4gms each above and below the standard. The test administration was carried out with this. The subject was asked to feel the standard weight. The test cylinder series was then given to the subject in one set of 2 minutes.The test cylinders were given and then the subject was asked to judge their weight while raising the cylinder to point one foot above the starting in a fixed time. The series was started from a weight judge as definitely heavier and lighter weights were given. The test was stopped after 2 minutes when the weights were judged as lighter twice in succession. The test was administered as above but the series was started from a weight judged as definitely lighter weight and will go on with increasing weights until the subject will judge the weights to be heavier twice in succession while lowering the cylinder from a point one feet above the end in a fixed time.

Statistical Design

The data obtained through test was compiled and tabulated. After the statistical analysis, the value of mean and standard deviation was computed and 't' test was applied to find out the significance of difference between the scores of winner- loser and male-female on perception variable. The study was tested at .05 level of significance.

Results and Discussions

Table 1

Mean difference in the scores of perception between Winners and Losers

STATUS	N	Mean	Std. Deviation	Std. Error Mean	T value	Remarks
Winners	80	4.03	1.763	.197	2.581	.011
Losers	80	3.39	1.331	.149		

In table 1, the mean value with SD and the computed 't' value on perception variable is presented. Results of the table 1 show that the winner group has recorded higher mean value (4.03) as compared to loser group mean value (3.39). The 't' value 2.581 has been found statistically significant at .05 level of confidence. Shown in table 1. However, from the results of this table, it can be deduced that winner group is having more perception than their counterpart's i.e. loser group. This might be possible due to the reason that while participating in various winning situations, the winners had to integrate various information and then had to decide appropriate action. A graphical presentation of the table 1 has been given in figure 1.

Figure 1

Mean scores of Perception Variable of Winners and Losers

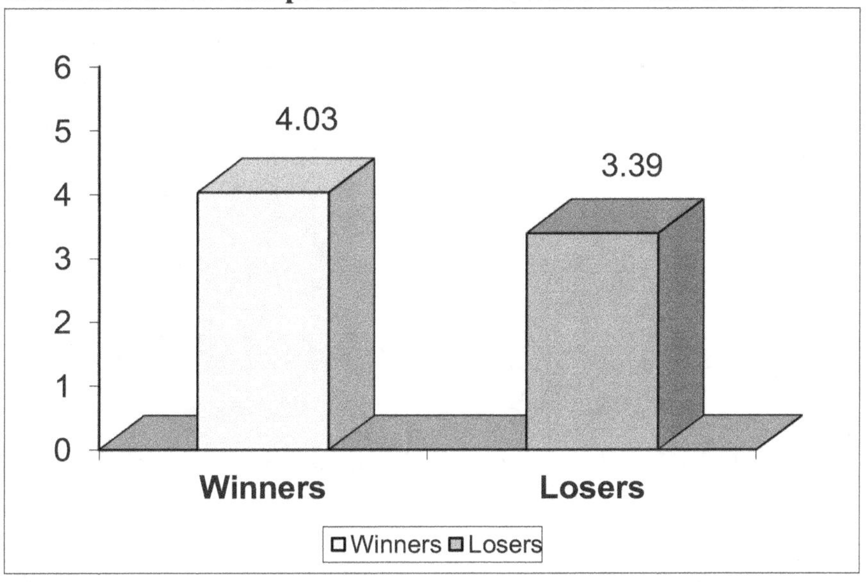

Table 2

Mean difference in the scores of perception between males and females

STATUS	N	Mean	Std. Deviation	Std. Error Mean	T value	Remarks
Males	80	3.93	1.661	.186	1.752	.082
Females	80	3.49	1.493	.167		

In table 2 are presented, the mean value with SD and the computed 't' value on perception variable. Results of the table 2 show that the male group has recorded higher mean value (3.93) as compared to female group mean value (3.49). The 't' value 1.752 shown in table 2 is found not significant at .05 level of confidence. Shown in figure 2.

Figure 2

Mean scores of Perception Variable of Males and Females

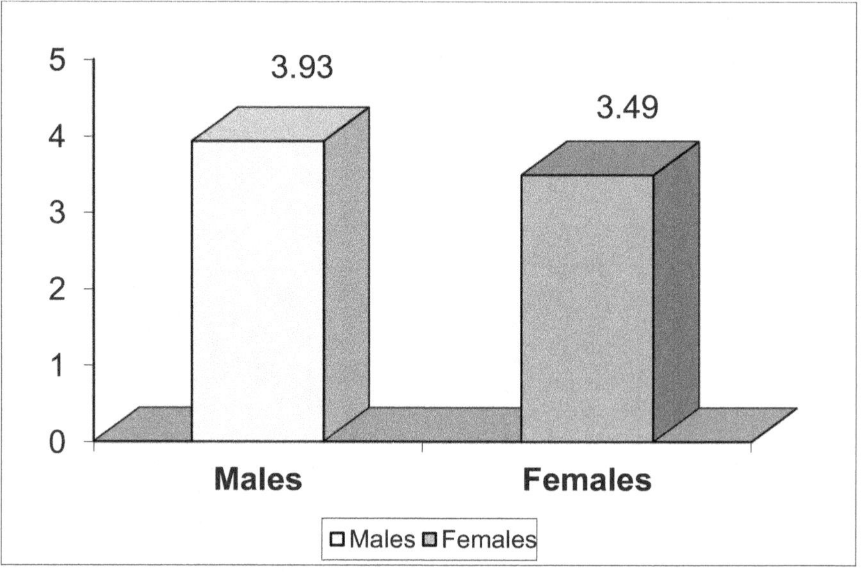

Conclusions

1. Winner and loser groups have significant difference on perception variable. However, winner group has recorded high mean value as their score, than the loser group. This is an indication that winner group has the better perception than the loser group.

2. Male and female groups have no significant difference on perception variable. However, male group has recorded high mean value as their score, than the female group. This indicates that male group has the better perception than the male group.

References

1. Brooks, J.E. Bulls, S.j. (2000). Derogation of student's female athlete who consult a sport psychologist on alternative perspective on the negative halo effect. Journal of winner's science and medicine in sport, Vol 4(1), March, 2001, pp.39-47.

2. Francoise Donchamps Riboux, Jean Karl Heinz and Jacques Douchamps (1989). Arousal as tri-dimensional variable: An exploratory study of behavioral changes in rowers following a marathon race. International Journal of sport psychology, Vol. 20, pp. 31-41.

3. Gould. D. Weiss, M. And Weinberg, R. (1982). Psychological characteristics of successful and non-successful big ten wrestlers. International Journal of Sport Psychology, 13:2.

4. Kathleen J. Hiscock, Merrill and Bergstrom, Canada (1988). Factors influencing ocular motility during the performance of cognitive tasks. Canadian Journal of Psychology, Vol. 42(1). 1-23.

5. Nideffer, R.M. (1976a). The inner athlete: Mind plus muscle for winning. New York Growell.

6. Singer, R.N. (1980). Motor learning and human performance. 3rd Ed. New York, Macmillian Co., p-249.

11

DIETRY AND PHYSICAL ACTIVITY COUNSELLING IN THE PREVENTION OF TYPE 2 DIABETES

Dr. Surjeet Singh [1]

Abstract

Type 2 diabetes, formerly known as non-insulin-dependent diabetes (NIDDM), constitutes a major portion (90-95%) of all cases of diabetes worldwide. The objective of this study was to evaluate and provide evidence on current published literature about diet and lifestyle in the prevention of type 2 diabetes and thereby making disease-specific recommendations. There is a convincing evidence for a decreased risk of type 2 diabetes in adults who are physically active and maintain their normal body mass index (BMI). Also an increased risk for developing type 2 diabetes is associated with overweight, obesity and physical inactivity. On the basis of available evidence regarding diet and lifestyle in the prevention of type 2 diabetes, it is recommended that a normal weight status in the lower BMI range (BMI 21–23) and regular physical activity be maintained throughout adulthood; abdominal obesity be prevented; and low intake of saturated be encouraged.

Key words: Type 2 diabetes, physical inactivity, obesity,

Introduction

Diabetes is a metabolic disease characterized by hyperglycemia (high blood sugar) resulting from defects in insulin secretion (Type 1 Diabetes),

---

[1] Sr. Assistant Professor, University of Kashmir, Srinagar

insulin action (Type 2 Diabetes) or both. It is associated with long-term damage, dysfunction, and failure of various organs, especially the eyes, kidneys, nerves, heart, and blood vessels.

The worldwide prevalence of diabetes is increasing at an alarming rate and is projected to increase by 48 % by the year 2030 (Canadian Diabetes Association Clinical Practice Guidelines Expert Committee, 2003). Inspite of the significant advances which have been made in the knowledge and management options for treating diabetes, it has become a pandemic disease (Flood & Constance, 2002). Type 2 Diabetes constitutes a major proportion (90-95%) of population diagnosed with diabetes, while 5- 10 % consist of Type 1 diabetes (National Institute of

Health, 2005). Type 2 Diabetes, which is most common, was figured at 150 million individuals in 2000 and this number was estimated to get double fold by 2025(King, Aubert & Herman, 1998). It is the fourth leading cause of deaths in most of developed countries. In rural areas its occurrence is little less because of prevalence of traditional life style (Amos, McCarty & Zimmet, 1997). In communities where there have occurred drastic changes in food habits from indigenous to a typical western diet, large incidences of type 2 diabetes have been observed for example , Aborigines in Australia, Pima Indians in Arizona (Bennett, 1999). The changes in the disease rates are attributed largely to the dietary as well as other life style factor more noticeably physical inactivity.

Prevalence of type 2 diabetes

In many parts of world especially the newly developing and industrialized countries, a dramatic increase has been observed in the incidences of type 2 Diabetes (King & Rewers, 1993). In coming future the most affected will be India and China (Table 1)

Table 1: Countries with Highest Number of Estimated Cases of Diabetes (in millions) for 2000 and 2030.[2]

Ranking	2000		2030	
	Country	People with diabetes	Country	People with diabetes
1	India	31.7	India	79.4
2	China	20.8	China	42.3
3	U.S.	17.7	U.S.	30.3
4	Indonesia	8.4	Indonesia	21.3
5	Japan	6.8	Japan	13.9
6	Pakistan	5.2	Pakistan	11.3
7	Russian Federation	4.6	Russian Federation	11.1
8	Brazil	4.6	Brazil	8.9
9	Italy	4.3	Italy	7.8
10	Bangladesh	3.2	Bangladesh	6.7
World Total (millions)	**177**			**366**

Adapted from Wild S et al. *Diabetes Care*, 2004.

The **366 million** figure which was estimated to reach by **2030** reached much earlier in **2011**. This shows the extent of pandemics of the diseases we are facing. Now by 2030, it has been estimated that it may reach to **552 million**.

Diabetes in India

No of adults with diabetes (million)		
2011	2030	
50.7	87.0	Shah et al., 2010. DRCP
61.3	101.2	Whiting et al 2011. DRCP

Figure 2. Populations in India

India has become the diabetes capital of the world (King. et al, 1998). The increase in number of diagnosed individuals mostly occurs in rapid urbanization areas and affects mostly the young age group as compared to the elders. In India, the complications of the disease are occurring earlier and progressing at dramatic rate. Further it is to mention that, there is more number of individuals who have diabetes but are not diagnosed than those of known ones.

Why to have a concern about the Diabetes.

Some of the facts which make it a real concern are that, every 3 seconds a person is diagnosed with diabetes, every 7 seconds a person dies from diabetes or related complications. Diabetes is the major cause of non traumatic lower limb amputations, largest cause of blindness. One in every three persons undergoing dialysis is affected with diabetes.

Complications.

i) Stroke:

A stroke happens when the blood supply to part of the brain is suddenly interrupted. Then brain tissue is damaged. In diabetic patients, the chances of having a stroke are twice higher than in people who don't have diabetes (Kannel, et al, 1990).

ii) Cardiovascular Disease:

Damage to the heart and blood vessels is collectively known as cardiovascular disease and people with diabetes have a higher chance of developing it. 8/10 individuals with diabetes die from CV events (Gray & Yudkin, 1997).

iii) Diabetic Neuropathy:

Diabetic neuropathy is a type of nerve damage that can occur due to diabetes. Diabetic neuropathy most often damages the nerves in legs and feet. It is the leading cause of non-traumatic lower extremity amputations (King, 1996)

iv) Diabetic Nephropathy:

Nephropathy means kidney disease or damage. Diabetic nephropathy is damage to kidneys caused by diabetes. It is the Leading cause of end-stage renal disease (Hypertens, 1993).

v) Diabetic Retinopathy:

Diabetic retinopathy affects eyes. It's caused by damage to the blood vessels of the light-sensitive tissue at the back of the eye (retina). It is the Leading cause of blindness in adults (UK Prospective Diabetes Study Group, 1990).

Modifiable risk factors

The section deals with the risk factors related   to dietary and life style factors. These factors play a significant role in the increased or decreased risk for the development of type 2 diabetes. These factors are modifiable i.e. can be modified in order to prevent the onset of the disease.

i) Obesity

Dieticians have developed a formula to calculate a number, called BMI (Body Mass Index) which is a measure of body fat based on height and weight that applies to adult men and women, **BMI = Weight/height (mt) ^{2}** . The following numbers are good indicators of whether are not you are overweight. Underweight = BMI of **19.8** or less, Normal Weight = BMI of **26.0,** Overweight = BMI of **26.0-29.0,** Obese = BMI over **29.0.** The obesity has made a drastic increase from past few years because of interaction between genetic and environmental factors (Kuczmarski , Flegal , Campbell & Johnson, 1994). The factors include: metabolic characteristics, physical inactivity, and habitual energy intake in relation to expenditure and macronutrient composition of the diet. The likelihood and severity of type 2 diabetes are closely linked with body mass index (BMI). There is a seven times greater risk of diabetes in obese people compared to those of healthy weight, with a threefold increase in risk for overweight people (Abdullah , Peeters & Courten ,2010). It has been observed that the rapid increase in the prevalence of type 2 diabetes from past few years among many populations is certainly related to increasing obesity. Further, data from the Nurses' Health Study has shown lower risk of diabetes occurs in the individuals who have BMI index nearing to

21, with the increase in this level, prevalence of obesity also increases (Colditz,et al, 1990).

ii) Physical inactivity

Because of increased prevalence of diabetes in the population, effective strategies and management is the need of hour. Physical activity along with diet and medication play a key role in the management of both type1 and type 2 diabetes (Sigal, Kenny, Wasserman, & Castaneda-Sceppa, 2004). Further, many other complications related with diabetes like cardiovascular diseases and cancer can be prevented through active participation in physical activities.

Despite of having known benefits of physical activities in relation with the prevention of diabetes, a large number of diabetic population are physically inactive. According to the report of (Plotnikoff, 2006), only about 36.3 and 28.1% adults in the population with type 1 and type 2 diabetes respectively are meeting the recommended physical activity guidelines i.e., 150 minutes/week of moderate physical exercises. So, there is a great need of developing the programmes which will help in promoting the physical activity among the diabetic patients of both the types. Recommendations with regard to physical activity as a preventative measure for developing type 2 diabetes are still difficult to quantify. However, more recent evidence suggests that vigorous exercise is required to improve insulin sensitivity (McAuley, 2002)

iii) Fat: quantity and quality

Both the quantity and quality of fats in the diet play a significant role in the modification of insulin sensitivity and glucose tolerance. A high intake of fats especially Trans fatty acids (TFAs), created through the transformation of polyunsaturated fatty acids which are abundant in western diets may promote insulin resistance and deterioration of glucose tolerance in our body. Several mechanism responsible for this deleterious effect of fats include, decreased binding of insulin to its receptors, reduced glucose transport, decreased glycogen synthesis and accumulation of stored triglycerides in skeletal muscles(Grundleger & Thenen,1982).

iv) Carbohydrates: quantity and quality

One area of confusion for diabetics and their diets is carbohydrates. So, should it be taken or eat avoided. Carbohydrates have a direct influence on blood sugar levels and so diets followed by people with diabetes tend to focus either on the quantity of carbohydrate intake or the speed at which carbohydrates are absorbed by the body.

Many controversies surround the optimal ratio of carbohydrate-to-fat in the diet with respect to the prevention of chronic diseases, including type 2 diabetes. A marked difference has been observed in different countries regarding this ratio. However, a positive association has been shown between the dietary fat intake and over-weight. This fact supports the notion of decreased fat intake but increased carbohydrate intake as a preventive measure for chronic diseases including type 2 diabetes (Marshall, Hamman & Baxter, 1991). Other studies (Salmeron, et al, 1997 & Meyer, et al, 2000) did not find any significant association between total carbohydrate consumption and diabetes risk. . It is known whenever a high carbohydrate intake takes place, an increased requirement for insulin secretion is felt in order to maintain glucose homeostasis. This process produces higher post-prandial (following a meal) insulin levels. It is possible that repeated stimulation of a high insulin secretion by a high carbohydrate diet could speed up an age-related decline in insulin secretion and lead to an earlier onset of type 2 diabetes (Grundy, 1999). The quality as well as the quantity of carbohydrates taken may however play a significant role in speeding up of this response. The most recent American dietary guidelines recommend intake of a variety of grain products (including whole grains) equating to six or more servings a day, however, no specific carbohydrate guideline, which is aimed at the prevention of type 2 diabetes is available. Therefore, a wide range of carbohydrate intakes may be acceptable in terms of achieving a low risk of type 2 diabetes with type and source of carbohydrate being more important than quantity.

Criteria for undergoing tests for pre-diabetes and diabetes in asymptomatic adults.

All the adults whose are over-weight (BMI 25 kg/m^2) and have additional risk factors discussed below should undergo testing for diabetes. The risk factors include: physical inactivity, first-degree relation with diabetic patient, member of high-risk ethnic group, women who delivers a baby weighing 9 lb, hypertension (140/90 mmHg), having HDL cholesterol level 35 mg/dl and/or a triglyceride level 250 mg/dl, women with polycystic ovarian syndrome, other clinical conditions associated with insulin resistance (e.g., severe obesity), history of CVD.

In the absence of the above criteria, testing for pre-diabetes and diabetes should begin at age 45 years. If results are normal, testing should be repeated at least at 3-year intervals, with consideration of more frequent testing depending on initial results and risk status.

Guidelines to regulate glycemic levels in relation to physical activity

Table 2- General guidelines of ADA/ACSM in regulating the glycemic response to physical activity

1. Metabolic control before physical activity.

- *Avoid physical activity if fasting glucose levels are >250 mg/dl and ketosis (abnormal fats) is present, and use caution if glucose levels are >300 mg/dl and no ketosis is present.*
- *Take additional carbohydrate if glucose levels are <100 mg/dl.*

2. Tracing blood glucose before and after physical activity.

- *Identify when changes in insulin or food intake are necessary.*
- *Learn the glycemic response to different physical activity conditions.*

3. Food intake

- *Consume added carbohydrate as needed to avoid hypoglycemia.*
- *Carbohydrate-based foods should be readily available during and after physical activity.*

Conclusion

The increased prevalence of type 2 disease from last few years has put a great cost on economic, social and personal factors among the people. Also, there is a great evidence regarding the prevention of type 2 diabetes through the implementation of life style measure like weight control and exercises. In order to achieve maximum benefits from these life style interventional measures (weight control & exercises), there must be change in government policies besides other community based programmes (Temple & Nestle 2001). The policy should include imparting nutrition education in schools, banning the advertisement of unhealthy products. Besides, stress should be laid on schools and other public health authorities to emphasize the role of weight control and increased physical activities in the prevention of type 2 diabetes. The priority should be given to Promotion and evaluation of 'healthy' lifestyle

Programmes, Healthy lifestyle programmes/interventions should focus on a life course perspective and not on a specific age group or developmental stage, Legislative action will be necessary to promote a healthier lifestyle for all populations.

References

1. Flood. L. & Constance. A. (2002). Diabetes and exercise safety. American Journal of Nursing, 102(6): 47-56.
2. Canadian Diabetes Association Clinical Practice Guidelines Expert Committee. (2003). Canadian diabetes association 2003 clinical practice guidelines for the prevention and management of diabetes in Canada. Canadian Journal of Diabetes, 27, s1–s140.

3. National Institute of Health. (2005). National diabetes statistics (Vol. 7).

4. King H., Aubert R.E, & Herman, W.H. (1998) Global burden of diabetes, 1995–2025: prevalence, numerical estimates, and projections. Diabetes Care, 21: 1414–31

5. Amos, A.F., McCarty, D.J., & Zimmet, P. (1997). The rising global burden of diabetes and its complications: estimates and projections, to the year 2010. Diabetic Medicine, 14: S7–85

6. Bennett, P.H.(1999). Type 2 diabetes among the Pima Indians of Arizona: an epidemic attributable to environmental change. Nutrition Reviews, 57: S51–4.

7. King H., Rewers, M. (1993). Global estimates for prevalence of diabetes mellitus and impaired glucose tolerance in adults. WHO Ad Hoc Diabetes Reporting Group. Diabetes Care,16: 157–77.

8. King H, et al. (1998). Diabetes Care, 21: 1414-1431

9. Shah, et al. (2010). *Diabetes Research* and *Clinical Practice.*

10. Whiting et al *Diabetes Research* and *Clinical Practice* 2011

11. Kannel, W.B, et al (1990). Am Heart J, 120:672–676

12. Gray, R.P ,& Yudkin, J.S. Cardiovascular disease in diabetes mellitus. In Textbook of Diabetes 2nd Edition, 1997. Blackwell Sciences.

13. King's Fund. (1996). Counting the cost. The real impact of non-insulin dependent diabetes. London: British Diabetic Association,

14. The Hypertension in Diabetes Study Group. (1993). *J Hypertens*, 11:309–317.

15. UK Prospective Diabetes Study Group. (1990). *Diabetes Research*, 13:1–11

16. Kuczmarski, R.J., Flegal, K.M., Campbell, S.M., & Johnson, C.L.(1994). Increasing prevalence of overweight among US adults. The National Health and Nutrition Examination Surveys, 160 NP Steyn et al.1960 to 1991. Journal of the American Medical Association, 273: 205–11.

17. Abdullah, A., Peeters, A., De Courten, M., et al. (2010). The magnitude of association between overweight and obesity and the risk of diabetes: a meta-analysis of prospective cohort studies. Diabetes Research & Clinical Practice, 89(3):309-19

18. Colditz, G.A., Willett, W.C., Stampfer, M..J, Manson, J.E., Hennekens, C.H., Arky R.A., & Speizer, F.E. (1990) Weight as a risk factor for clinical diabetes in women. American Journal of Epidemiology, 132: 501–13.

19. Sigal, R.J., Kenny, G.P., Wasserman, D.H., & Castaneda-Sceppa, C. (2004). Physical activity/ exercise and type 2 diabetes. Diabetes Care, 27, 2518–2539.

20. Plotnikoff, R.C. (2006). Physical activity in the management of diabetes: Population-based issues and approaches. Canadian Journal of Diabetes, 30, 52–62.

21. McAuley, K.A., Williams, S.M., Mann, J.I., Goulding, A., Chisholm, A., Wilson, N., Story, G., McLay, R.T., Harper, M.J.,& Jones, I.E. (2002) Intensive lifestyle changes are necessary to improve insulin sensitivity: a randomized controlled trial. Diabetes Care, 25: 445–52.

22. Grundleger, M.L, & Thenen, S.W. (1982). Decreased insulin binding, glucose transport, and glucose metabolism in soleus muscle of rats fed a high fat diet. Diabetes, 31: 232–7.

23. Marshall, J.A., Hamman, R.F., & Baxter, J. (1991). High-fat, low carbohydrate diet and the aetiology of non-insulin dependent diabetes mellitus: the San Luis Valley Diabetes Study. American Journal of Epidemiology, 134: 590–603.

24. Salmeron, J., Manson, J.E., Stampfer, M..J, Colditz, G.A., Wing, A.L.,& Willett, W.C.(1997). Dietary fiber, glycemic load, and risk of noninsulin- dependent diabetes mellitus in women. Journal of the American Medical Association, 277: 472–7.

25. Meyer, K.A., Kushi, L.H., Jacobs, D.R., Slavin, J., Sellers, T.A., & Folsom, A.R. (2000). Carbohydrates, dietary fiber, and incident type 2 diabetes in older women. American Journal of Clinical Nutrition, 71: 921–30.

26. Grundy SM. The optimal ratio of fat-to-carbohydrate in the diet. (1999). Annual Review of Nutrition, 19: 325–41.

27. Temple, N.J., & Nestle, M. (2001). Population nutrition, health promotion and government policy. In: Wilson T, Temple NJ, eds. Nutritional Health: Strategies for Diseases Prevention. Totowa, NJ: Humana, 13–29.